```
571     Quennell, Marjorie
Q          (Courtney)

        Everyday life in
          prehistoric times
```

DATE			

AKIBA-SCHECHTER DAY SCHOOL
5200 Hyde Park Boulevard
Chicago, Illinois 60615

© THE BAKER & TAYLOR CO.

EVERYDAY LIFE
IN
PREHISTORIC TIMES

Frontispiece

1   Magdalenian Painting

EVERYDAY LIFE
IN
PREHISTORIC TIMES

By
MARJORIE & C. H. B. QUENNELL

LONDON: B. T. BATSFORD LTD
NEW YORK: G. P. PUTNAM'S SONS

Revised Edition © Marjorie Quennell, 1959

TO
E.R.Q.
&
H.Q.

*First published as "Everyday Life in the Old Stone Age"
and "Everyday Life in the New Stone Age"
Fifth Editions, 1955
First published, revised in one volume, 1959
Fifth impression, 1968
ISBN 0 7134 1673 4
Reprinted 1973*

PRINTED IN GREAT BRITAIN BY FLETCHER AND SON LTD, NORWICH
AND BOUND BY RICHARD CLAY (THE CHAUCER PRESS) LTD, BUNGAY, SUFFOLK
FOR THE PUBLISHERS
B. T. BATSFORD LTD, 4 FITZHARDINGE STREET, PORTMAN SQUARE, LONDON, W.1
G. P. PUTNAM'S SONS, 200 MADISON AVENUE, NEW YORK, N.Y. 10016

Books by the Quennells

EVERYDAY LIFE IN PREHISTORIC TIMES

EVERYDAY LIFE IN ROMAN AND ANGLO-SAXON TIMES

EVERYDAY THINGS IN ANCIENT GREECE

A HISTORY OF EVERYDAY THINGS IN ENGLAND

    VOLUME I. FROM 1066 TO 1499

    VOLUME II. FROM 1500 TO 1799

    VOLUME III. FROM 1733 TO 1851

    VOLUME IV. FROM 1851 TO 1914

"The operations of the mind no doubt find their noblest expression in the language of speech, yet they are also eloquent in the achievements of the hand. The works of man's hands are his embodied thought, they endure after his bodily framework has passed into decay, and thus throw a welcome light on the earliest stages of his unwritten history."

From *Ancient Hunters* by Prof. W. J. SOLLAS

PREFACE

THIS little book has come into being as a result of another that we wrote and illustrated. It was intended for boys and girls, and we called it a *History of Everyday Things in England*. An attempt was made to draw the eyes of our readers away from the Destruction which was to the fore in those days, and to present instead a picture of all the care and trouble which had gone to the Construction of the everyday things that were being destroyed. We gave the matter very careful consideration, and it seemed to us essential that the things illustrated should be of a type with which our readers would be familiar. Boys and girls, in their summer holidays, might have seen the Norman work at Norwich or Castle Rising, or the Renaissance work of Inigo Jones at Raynham. With some reluctance we made no mention of any earlier work. The doings of Roman, Saxon, and Dane were only hinted at, and the prehistoric period was not mentioned at all. We started with William the Conqueror, and finished at the start of the twentieth century.

Since we appear to have interested many boy and girl readers, we now want to fill in the long space before 1066. One is so apt to lump together all the earlier work, and think of it as having been done in a few centuries; the sense of perspective is lost. History is rather like travelling on the railway, the events flash past like telegraph posts, the nearer ones having their due spaces in between; but if we look back, the events, like the posts, are all bunched together and we cannot realize the spaces.

These spaces are as important as the events of History, and represent the periods when people were making up their minds; recovering perhaps from great disasters, or gathering their forces to go forward.

The races of mankind, like their works, develop by growth to flower and decay, but always there is a re-birth or renaissance. The Madeleine Art we illustrate died out in 12,000 B.C., yet still lives to inspire us; that is the boys and girls who want to do work, because if History is divided into events, and spaces, then the people are divided into those who have ideas, and want to do and make things, and the others who only deal in the ideas, and benefit by them.

Personally we hold that History is not just dates, but a long tale of man's life, labour, and achievement; and if this be so, we cannot afford to neglect the doings of prehistoric men, who with flint for

PREFACE

their material, made all the implements and weapons they needed for their everyday life.

We call the pick-and-shovel historian an Archaeologist, from the Greek *archaios*, ancient, and *logos*, discourse. The archaeologist is helped by the astronomers and mathematicians, who are called in to decide in matters of climatic change like the Glacial Periods. A skull is found, like the one at Swanscombe in Kent, and the anatomists examine it carefully to fit it into its place as a link in the chain of man's development. The science of man and mankind is called Anthropology, from *anthropos*, a man, and *logos*, discourse. The science of life is Biology. One must also know something of geology, which is the science that deals with the structure of the earth.

Many books have been written on Prehistoric Archaeology but these are on the whole not suitable for boys and girls. We have therefore taken the ascertained and proved facts, and have plotted these out as a plan. If our readers are interested in this plan they can themselves raise a superstructure of more advanced knowledge. We do not lay claim to any great store of archaeological knowledge ourselves, and have approached our task rather as illustrators. As painter and architect, who have been making things ourselves all our lives, we may perhaps be able to treat the work of prehistoric man in a sympathetic fashion, and hope our pictures will help boys and girls to *see* these old people a little.

This brings up the question of how we are to approach prehistoric man. We must free our minds of prejudice. Some people will say that he was a loathsome creature, incredibly dirty and unpleasant. Obviously this could not have been the case with the Madeleine people, whose work we see on p. 100. There will be other people who will regard our friend as the Noble Savage, and clothe him in their minds with all the simple virtues. It will not do to jump to conclusions. Shall we judge him by his *work*? If we try to find out how he lived, the tools he used, and the things that he made with them, then in the end we shall have a picture in our own minds. This is the essential part of reading a book, that it should help us to form our own conclusions. So we do not seek to teach, nor do we wish to preach, but we do want to interest our readers, and here we give you fair warning. If we can do so; if this subtle little microbe can work its way into your system, and you want to find out how things were made and done, then you may become archaeologists yourselves.

MARJORIE AND C. H. B. QUENNELL

CONTENTS

	Page
PREFACE	9
ACKNOWLEDGMENT	13
LIST OF ILLUSTRATIONS	15
BIBLIOGRAPHY	20

Chapter

		Page
I	HOW TO DATE BY GEOLOGY	23
II	THE EARLIEST MEN OF THE OLD STONE AGE	34
III	THE FIRST CAVE-DWELLERS	57
IV	ARTISTS OF THE OLD STONE AGE	72
	Aurignac Man	72
	Solutré Man	86
	Madeleine Man	88
V	THE MESOLITHIC PERIOD OR THE END OF THE OLD STONE AGE	106
VI	THE NEW STONE AGE	115
VII	THE BRONZE AGE	149
VIII	THE EARLY IRON AGE	181
	INDEX	221

ACKNOWLEDGMENT

The Authors and Publishers wish to thank the following for permission to reproduce the illustrations appearing in this book:

Major G. W. G. Allen, for fig. 138.

American School of Prehistoric Research, Peabody Museum, Harvard University, for fig. 66 (from *La Colombière Report* by Sheldon Judson and Hallam L. Movius).

The Trustees of the British Museum, for figs. 78 and 136.

Hull Municipal Museums, for fig. 132 (from the exhibit in the Mortimer Archaeological Collection at Hull).

Illustrated London News and Brian Hope-Taylor, F.S.A., for fig. 79.

The Ministry of Works, for fig. 67, crown copyright, reproduced by permission of the Controller of H.M. Stationery Office.

National Museum, Denmark, for figs. 130, 131 and 135.

National Museum of Wales, for figs. 133 and 134.

Dr. J. K. St. Joseph, for fig. 137.

Schweiz. Landesmuseum, Zürich, for fig. 77.

They must also acknowledge the sources of the new line illustrations which are included in this edition:

Fig. 8 is reproduced from *Ancient Stone Implements of the British Isles* by John Evans; fig. 9 from *Man the Tool Maker* by K. P. Oakley (British Museum Natural History publication); figs. 10-13 from *The Sturge Collection* by R. A. Smith (British Museum publication); figs. 34 and 35 from *Le Préhistorique* by A. de Mortillet; figs. 36, 37 and 43-6 from *The Rock Shelter of La Colombière*, all by S. Judson and H. L. Movius; fig. 52 after E. Cartailhac; fig. 61 from *La Caverne de Niaux* by H. Breuil; fig. 62 after E. Piette; fig. 63 after E. Ray Lankester; figs. 64 and 65 from *Catalogue of Stone Age Antiquities in the British Museum*; figs. 70-2 from *Fossil Man in Spain* by H. Obermier, New Haven, 1925 (Yale University Press); fig. 73 from *Préhistoire de la Mediterranée* by M. Sauter; fig. 84 from *Jungsteinzeitseidlungen in Federseemoor* by R. R. Schmidt; fig. 86 from V. G. Childe in *Proc. Preh. Soc.* 1949, 77; figs. 87 and 88 after Vassits in *Prehist. Zeit.* 1910; fig. 105 from *Woodhenge* by M. and E. Cunnington (Devizes Museum publication); fig. 116 from *Urgeschichte der Bildenden Kunst in Europa* by H. Hoernes; fig. 119 from *Manuel de L'Archeologie Préhistorique* by J. Dechelette; fig. 120 from *Le Char et le traneau* by H. Breuil; fig. 123 from *A Guide to the Prehistoric Rock Engravings* by C. Bicknell; figs. 127-9 after W. J. Hemp; figs. 144, 156 and 159 from *Prehistoric Europe* by J. G. D. Clark (Methuen and Co. Ltd., 1950).

LIST OF ILLUSTRATIONS

The numerals in parentheses in the text refer to the *figure numbers* of the illustrations

Figure		Page
1	Magdalenian painting	Frontispiece
2	Causes of the Ice Ages	24
3	Glaciers and moraines	27
4	The formation of river terraces	29
5	The Farnham Terraces	32
6	Lower Palaeolithic man makes a flint implement	35
7	Making fire	36
8	Flint implement found near Gray's Inn Lane in the seventeenth century	37
9	How a flake is knocked off a flint hand-axe	38
10	Front and side view of an Abbevillian hand-axe	38
11	Front and side view of an early (Abbevillian) hand-axe	39
12	Front and side view of an Acheulean hand-axe (cleaver variety)	40
13	Front and side view of an Acheulean hand-axe (ovate variety)	41
14	Lower Palaeolithic scraper	42
15	*Machairodus*, the sabre-toothed tiger	43
16	The pitfall	44
17	Falling spear	45
18	A wind-break	46
19	*Elephas primigenius*, the mammoth	47
20	*Rhinoceros tichorhinus*, the woolly-coated rhinoceros	48
21	Pithecanthropus—the Java Ape-man	49
22	A bark raft	53
23	Making grass rope	54
24	Moustier cave-dwellers	58
25	Poise of the Neanderthal figure	59
26	Moustier spear-head	61
27	Australian spear-throwing	62
28	Australian spear-throwing	63
29	Hafting	64
30	Australian hut	64

LIST OF ILLUSTRATIONS

Figure		Page
31	Making fire	65
32	A bark canoe	66
33	A primitive spindle	68
34	Blade cores	73
35	Flint blades	74
36	Two flint burins, chisels or gravers	75
37	Two flint burins, chisels or gravers	75
38	Type of huts suggested by Aurignac drawings	76
39	The spokeshave	77
40	Shaft straightening	78
41	The bow-drill	79
42	Aurignac drawing	81
43–6	An Aurignacian artist's sketch-book on a stone, with three of the sketches drawn out separately	82–3
47	Solutré flints	86
48	Making of bone needles	87
49	Magdalenian portrait of a woman	88
50	Spears and harpoons	90
51	A man diving into a river. Engraved on a Magdalenian bone tool	91
52	Magdalenian engravings on bones of seals and fish	92
53	The kayak	93
54	Framework of kayak	94
55	Eskimo bladder dart, harpoon, and bird dart	94
56	Eskimo game	95
57	Type of huts suggested by Madeleine drawings	96
58	Type of hut suggested by Madeleine drawings	97
59	Eskimo summer tent	97
60	Digging-stick	98
61	A wall painting of a bison	98
62	The head of a galloping horse	99
63	Deer crossing a stream. Engraved on a round bone	100
64	Three horses swimming across a stream. Engraved on a flat rib-bone	101
65	A Magdalenian artist's sketch-book	101
66	A Palaeolithic rock shelter	103
67	A Neolithic religious sanctuary at Avebury	104
68	Chisel-ended arrow-heads	107
69	Mas d'Azil painted pebbles	107

LIST OF ILLUSTRATIONS

Figure		Page
70	A deer hunt	109
71	A man chasing two stags	110
72	A woman gathering honey	111
73	Wall painting of an ibex	112
74	Danish midden axe	113
75	Dug-out canoe	116
76	Reconstruction of an Iron Age hill fort	119
77	Neolithic weaving pattern from the Swiss Lakes	121
78	Bronze Age face ornament	121
79	A gold breastplate of the Bronze Age	122
80	Flint miners	125
81	Hafting of flint implements	126
82	Stone axes and hammers	126
83	Flint spear- and arrow-heads	128
84	Plan of a Neolithic house at Aichbuhl	129
85	Aichbuhl Neolithic village	130
86	A Neolithic dolls' house	130
87	Plan of a clay oven	131
88	A clay oven	131
89	Strike-a-light	132
90	A flint sickle	132
91	Grinding corn	133
92	Pounding grain	133
93	Making pottery	134
94	Pottery spoon	135
95	Earth house, Usinish, South Uist, Hebrides	137
96	Picts house, Sutherland (Iron Age)	138
97	Eskimo rock hut	139
98	Eskimo snow house	139
99	Picts tower (Iron Age)	140
100	A cromlech or dolmen	140
101	A standing stone	141
102	The laws of leverage	142
103	Builders at work	143
104	Stonehenge	145
105	Plan of "Woodhenge", Salisbury Plain	147
106	Development of Bronze axe	151
107	Hafting of palstave and socketed axe	152
108	Development of Bronze spear	153

LIST OF ILLUSTRATIONS

Figure   *Page*

Figure		Page
109	A leaf-shaped sword	153
110	A Bronze Age smith	154
111	Bronze brooch and pin	156
112	Spinning	156
113	Warp-weighted loom of simplest type	157
114	Warp-weighted loom of more developed type	158
115	A comb	159
116	Bronze Age drawing of women weaving	159
117	Shaving with Bronze razor	160
118	Wooden wheels	161
119	A funeral procession engraved on a piece of broken pottery	162
120	A rock engraving of two chariots	162
121	A clapper bridge	163
122	A plough	164
123	Rock engraving of a man ploughing with oxen	165
124	Bronze Age pottery ornament	166
125	Bronze Age pottery	167
126	Bronze Age barrows	168
127	Plan of the chambered cairn of Bryn Celli Dhu, Anglesey	170
128	Diagram of markings on the pattern stone, Bryn Celli Dhu	171
129	Pillar stone in chamber of Bryn Celli Dhu	171
130	Bronze Age clothing: female	173
131	Bronze Age clothing: male	173
132	Bronze Age toy boat	174
133	Bronze Age ship bowl	174
134	Underside of ship with sea-waves and ship's eyes	174
135	Iron Age man	183
136	Celtic shield from Battersea	183
137	Celtic fields	184
138	Celtic hill figure at Uffington	184
139	Glastonbury lake village	186
140	Hut interior at Glastonbury	188
141	Hut sections	189
142	Building a hut at Glastonbury	190
143	Dug-out canoe and landing-stage at Glastonbury	191
144	Rock engraving of two men fishing from a boat	192

LIST OF ILLUSTRATIONS

Figure		Page
145	Grinding corn	193
146	Smelting iron	194
147	Saw and adze	195
148	An iron knife	196
149	Penannular brooch	196
150	Brooches and brooch springs	197
151	A pole lathe	199
152	A dew pond	204
153	Coracles	206
154	Framework of umiak	207
155	Eskimo umiak	208
156	Rock engraving of two Bronze or Iron Age war vessels	208
157	Early Iron Age swords and spears	209
158	Enamelled harness ornament	209
159	Two Scythian men wearing trousers, drawn on an Iron Age vessel	210
160	The Bronze mirror	211
161	A potter's wheel	212
162	Celtic patterns	213
163	Currency bars	216

BIBLIOGRAPHY

EARLY MEN

Burkitt, M. C., *The Old Stone Age* (Cambridge, 1958).

Clark, Grahame, *From Savagery to Civilization* (Cressett Press, 1947).

Coon, C. P., *Up From the Ape*.

Coon, C. P., *Why Men behave like Apes and vice-versa*.

Lamming, Annette, *Lascaux* (Penguin Books, 1959).

Leahey, L. S. B., *Adam's Ancestors* (Methuen, 1953).

Oakley, K. P., *Man the Toolmaker* (Natural History Museum, 1958).

Watson, William, *Flint Implements* (British Museum, 1959).

GENERAL PREHISTORY

Childe, V. G., *What Happened in History* (Penguin Books, 1942).

Childe, V. G., *Man Makes Himself* (Oxford, 1956).

Clark, Grahame, *Archaeology and Society* (Methuen, 1956).

Clark, Grahame, *An Outline of World Prehistory* (Cambridge, 1961).

Coon, C. P., *The Races of Europe* (Macmillan, 1939).

Davies, G. E., *The Megalith Builders of Western Europe* (Hutchinson, 1958).

LATER PREHISTORIC TIMES IN BRITAIN

Atkinson, R. J. C., *Stonehenge* (Hamilton, 1956, Penguin Books, 1960).

BIBLIOGRAPHY

Bruce-Nutford, R., *Recent Archaeological Excavations in Britain* (Routledge, 1954).

Bulleid, A., *The Lake Villages of Somerset.*

Childe, V. G., *The Prehistory of Scotland* (Cambridge, 1935).

Clark, Grahame, *Prehistoric England* (Batsford, 1940).

Clarke, R. Rainbird, *East Anglia* (Thames & Hudson, 1959).

Fox, Sir Cyril, *The Personality of Britain* (Cardiff, National Museum of Wales, 1959).

Fox, Sir Cyril, *A Find of the Early Iron Age from Llyn Cerrig* (Cardiff, National Museum of Wales).

Fox, Sir Cyril, *Life and Death in the Bronze Age* (Routledge, 1959).

Grimes, W. F., *The Prehistory of Wales* (Cardiff, National Museum of Wales, 1951).

Hawkes, Jacquetta, *Early Britain* (Collins, 1944).

Hawkes, Jacquetta and Christopher, *Prehistoric Britain* (Chatto, 1947, Penguin Books, 1949).

Piggott, Stuart, *Britain in Prehistory* (Oxford, 1949).

Piggott, Stuart, *Scotland Before History.*

O'Riordan, Sean, *Antiquities of the Irish Countryside* (Methuen, 1953).

Raftery, Joseph, *Prehistoric Ireland* (Batsford, 1951).

Stone, J. F. S., *Wessex Before the Celts* (Thames & Hudson, 1958).

GUIDE BOOKS

Hawkes, J. J., *A Guide to the Prehistoric and Roman Monuments in Britain and Wales* (Chatto, 1951).

Sieveking, Ann & G. de G., *A Short Guide to Caves of France and Northern Spain* (Vista Books, 1961).

Thomas, Nicholas, *A Guide to Prehistoric England* (Batsford, 1960).

Chapter I

HOW TO DATE BY GEOLOGY

WE said in our Introduction that the archaeologist is a pick-and-shovel historian. He investigates the lives of the ancient peoples by the remains which they have left behind them; he needs must dig for his information, because the very earliest times are prehistoric, and no written word remains.

When the archaeologist digs up some ancient remains, for example a single grave, or the buried foundations of a house, he may be certain that all the things in his excavation belong together. In the case of a grave they may all have belonged to a single person. This is what archaeologists call an "association". All the objects found in the grave are truly associated with one another in the archaeological sense. They are probably all of the same date, though some of the most beautifully made objects may be heirlooms inherited by the dead man from his father or even his grandfather. In modern times graves have gravestones with dates written upon them, and often you will see the date when a house was built carved upon it in the same manner as on a gravestone. There are all sorts of other ways in which graves or houses may be dated in historic times. They may contain coins, which can be dated accurately, or hall-marked silver, or fragments of pottery marked with the name of the maker. In the later prehistoric periods of Europe, the Neolithic, the Bronze Age, the Iron Age, similar methods can be used, for the "association" may contain an imported piece coming from thousands of miles away, from the ancient civilizations of the Near East and of Greece and Rome where there lived people who could read and write and calculate in terms of years. These imports—perhaps they are glass beads or wine vessels—can be dated by the archaeologist and so used to date the "association" and perhaps a whole prehistoric people using the same sort of things as were found in the grave.

During the earliest period of Man's existence, which we call the Old Stone Age, nobody could read or write. The men of the Old Stone Age may have calculated in seasons, or even in

HOW TO DATE BY GEOLOGY

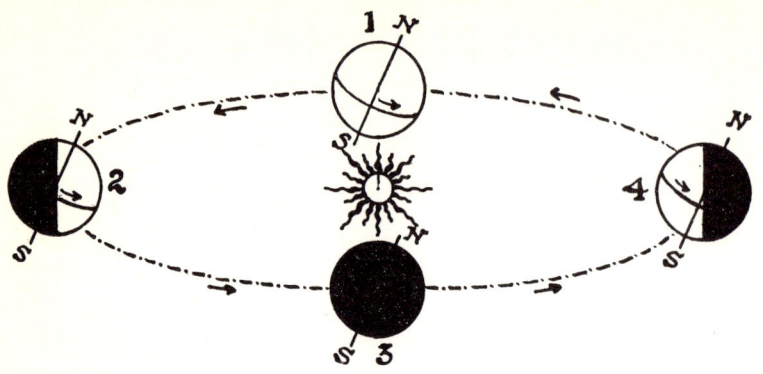

2   Causes of the Ice Ages

months, from the waning of one moon to the next, but they had no means of recording their calculations.

So, when the archaeologist wishes to know how old a flint implement, or an "association", may be he has to ask the scientist to find him a new way to calculate. Luckily for us, throughout the whole of the period of the Old Stone Age, perhaps half a million years or more, the world's climate was constantly changing from very hot to very cold, and back again. These changes are recorded in the earth's surface and geologists can date the deposits in which the changes are recorded, relative to each other, so that when we can find a stone tool in these deposits we can give it a geological date.

We must now discuss these changes in climate. They are sometimes spoken of as the Ice Age, a period when the climate of England was much colder than it is now, when the polar ice covered not only Scandinavia, but the North Sea and all of Scotland and Northern England. Actually, however, there were four Ice Ages, all of them tens of hundreds of thousands of years long, and separated from each other by periods just as long when the climate in England was hotter than it is today and hippopotami swam in the Thames. How did this come about?

We all know that the earth revolves round the sun on a path which is called its orbit. It completes the circle in a year, and turns on its own axis in so doing once a day, or 365 times in the year. As the earth turns round on its axis, the part which is

PRECESSION OF THE EQUINOXES

towards the sun enjoys daylight, and in the part which is away it is the night.

It is quite a good plan to make a rough working model of all this on a table, as fig. 2, and a globe will help; or let an orange take the place of the earth, and drive a knitting-needle through it for the axis. A candle in the middle of the table can be the sun. If the table is circular, the edge can be the earth's orbit; if not, a circle can be drawn in chalk. If, on this path, the knitting-needle is placed in a vertical position, so that the equator of the orange, or earth, is level with the candle, or sun, then it can be seen that the equator will derive more light from the candle than the top and bottom where the knitting-needle comes through. So we discover in the case of the earth, that the equator is hotter than the polar caps, because it gets more sunshine. If we move the orange round the orbit, turning it as we go, but keeping the knitting-needle upright, we arrive at day and night, heat and cold, but not summer and winter, or why, when we have summer, Australia has winter; but let the knitting-needle lean over, and we have an entirely different state of affairs. This is what has happened, and today the angle of inclination of the equator to the orbit of the earth is 23° 27'. Fig. 2 shows how this affects the seasons.

The Vernal Equinox of March 21st is shown at position 1, when day and night are equal. At the Summer Solstice on June 21st, position 2, all the North Hemisphere will be turned towards the sun, and we get the longest days. At the Autumnal Equinox, September 23rd, position 3, day and night are again equal. The Winter Solstice, position 4, comes on December 21st with the shortest day, and the Northern Hemisphere leans away from the sun and warmth.

This inclination of the equator to the earth's orbit, through long ages, varies from 22° 6' to 24° 50'. The former would give us less difference between winter and summer than we have now, the latter would increase the difference. The shape of the earth's orbit changes, and sometimes is roughly elliptical, with the sun much nearer to one end than the other. This would mean short summers and long cold winters.

This is what is called the Precession of the Equinoxes; the earth wobbles as it spins, and this further affects the inclination of the axis. The Gulf Stream now gives us a better climate than

HOW TO DATE BY GEOLOGY

that to which our latitude entitles us. When we bear in mind that a very small fall in the temperature would bring back the snow and ice, then it is easy to see how a combination of the conditions we have mentioned may have caused the Ice Ages.

There is no need for alarm—thousands of years pass as the earth slowly wobbles on its journey.

The existence of these former Ice Ages was realized when geologists first began to study the places which are still in an Ice Age today, such as Switzerland. The geologists soon realized that the conditions in Switzerland had parallels in places where there is no ice today—so in order to understand the geological dating of Old Stone Age man we must go and study the glaciers in Switzerland.

A glacier is a very slowly moving river of ice. Gathering its forces from the snowfields on the summits of the mountains, it moves by gravity down the valleys, and collects tributaries as it goes along. In doing this the snow solidifies into ice, and it is quite easy to see that a tremendous pressure must be exercised on the sides of the valleys. If we go into a mountainous region, which during the Ice Age had glaciers, we shall find plenty of evidence of their existence. The sides of the valleys have been worn smooth by the slowly moving mass of ice grinding into the rocks (*roches moutonnées*); there will also be piles of splintered rocks which are called moraines. The intense cold causes the rocks above the valley to crack and splinter, and fragments fall and are left as embankments at the sides, or rolling on to the ice are carried along. These are called lateral moraines(*3*, 1). Where two glaciers join, these meet, and flowing down the middle of the lower glaciers are called medial moraines(*3*, 2). In this way glaciers transport materials for long distances. The débris of the lateral moraines falls into crevasses, or cracks in the ice, and appears lower down in the terminal moraines.

The glacier moving downhill, comes to a place where the temperature is warmer, and the ice melts. Here we find what is called a terminal moraine or moraine girdle(*3*, 3). These are generally fan-shaped, and represent the heap of broken rock and stone, which has been pushed forward under the snout of the glacier, and gathered up by it in its progress from the bed and sides of the valley. The existence of old moraine girdles, which have become covered with soil and trees, and now look like hills,

3 Glaciers and moraines

HOW TO DATE BY GEOLOGY

is a proof of ice conditions in former times. There are girdle moraines as far west as Lyons in France, which prove that the Swiss glaciers were once of enormous length. High up on the sides of valleys, the *roches moutonnées* show that the glaciers were once very much deeper. All these facts help the scientists in their conclusions as to the duration of the Ice Ages, and the temperature then general.

Behind a moraine girdle, in the bed of the old glacier, we find a sort of enormous basin, filled with hummocks of boulder clay, called drumlins, at 4. To make this apparent the ice of the glacier has been broken away at 5. This clay is the mud which was brought down by the glacier, and was formed by the churning action of its underside on the rocks over which it passed.

Below the moraine girdle, we find what the Germans call Schotter fields. It is here, where the ice melts, that the river comes into being, carrying away the smaller pieces of rock, depositing them first in the schotter, then breaking and rolling the pieces until lower down we find them in the gravel formations of the river terraces. Our readers, perhaps, will know a river whose banks descend in terraced steps; it is a very usual formation. This connection between the glaciers, their girdle moraines, and river terraces is very important, because by their aid men like Professors Geikie and Penck have worked out the theory of the Glacial Periods.

Professor Penck studied the River Steyr in Upper Austria, and found that each of its terraces connected up with the girdle moraine of an ancient glacier, and from this the following theory of the formation of terraces themselves has been evolved. Fig. *4* has been prepared to illustrate this.

Bed A in fig. *4* would be pre-glacial. In the First Glacial Period, at the end of Pliocene times, the volume of water in the rivers would not have been large, because so much was locked up in the ice of the glaciers.

Then came the warmer weather of the First Interglacial Period, when vast quantities of water were melted out of the glaciers, and hurrying down the old river bed, or forming another, cut a new channel to B. As the water lost its power to cut channels it began to build up the bed of gravel at C.

Then came the Second Glacial Period, and the river again shrank in size. At the Second Interglacial Period the bed was cut

RIVER TERRACES

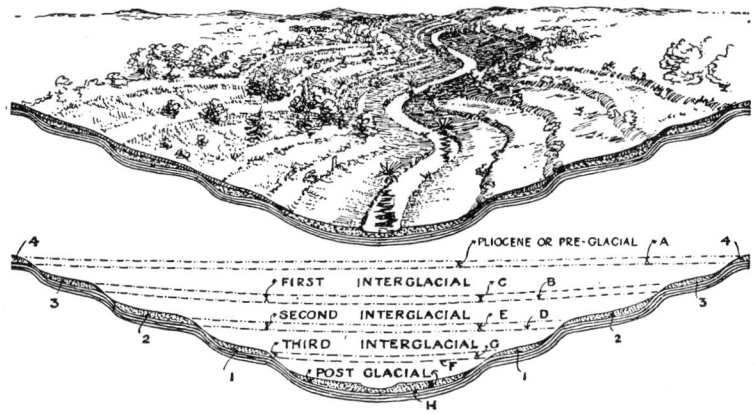

4 The Formation of river terraces

down to D, and the bed of gravel at E built up gradually afterwards. The channel was cut down to F in Third Interglacial times, and bed G formed, and the final channel H cut in the warmer times after the Fourth Glacial Period, which we call post-glacial.

To revert to the theory of how the terraces 1, 2, and 3 were formed, we have shown the gravels of which they are composed by a dotted surface, and it will be seen that they are in reality the edges of old river-beds, which have been left behind as the water cut its way down.

Fig. 4 can be taken as showing the terraces of the Somme at St. Acheul. The Somme is celebrated, because it was here, at Abbeville, in the middle of the nineteenth century, that M. Boucher de Perthes discovered large quantities of flint implements in the gravel deposits.

At the time when this discovery was made we did not know much about the formation of river terraces, but it was realized that these flint implements must be very old indeed because they were associated in the gravels with the bones of extinct animals. As the stone tools were recognized as made by man this meant that man was himself much older than everyone thought. So that it was of great importance to date the river terraces where these stone tools had been found.

It will perhaps be as well for us now to run through the implements found in the terraces of the Somme(4), because it

HOW TO DATE BY GEOLOGY

will familiarize our readers with the recognized French names for the various divisions of the Old Stone Age. We have no corresponding English names, so the French ones have been very generally adopted, and these are the names of places where typical implements have been found.

No implements have been found in terraces 3 and 4, which leads us to suppose that man did not live on the banks of the Somme before the Second Interglacial Period. In the next terrace downwards, No. 2, Abbevillian implements are found. We shall explain what these are later; meanwhile, how did they get there? We have imagined a mighty river rushing down in flood at the beginning of the Second Interglacial Period, when the tremendous glaciers began to shrink and melt away, and this would be quite a different matter to the wastage only, which went on during glacial times. This flood of water is not an exaggeration. Remember that we are writing about periods which extended over, not hundreds, but thousands of years; also that we are living in an interglacial period now. In September 1920 a warm spell of a few days, accompanied by rain after a rather cold summer, caused a serious situation at Chamonix in Switzerland. The papers said a glacier had "burst". What really happened was that the rise in temperature caused the Mont Anvers Glacier to melt more rapidly than its accustomed rate of wastage. Masses of ice broke away, and were swept with stone and mud into the valley. Rivers rose, trees were uprooted, and houses carried away. Now think of the whole of the north of Europe under an ice-cap, and the Swiss glaciers extending as far west as Lyons in France, and the temperature gradually becoming warmer. The scientists tell us that it only wants a fall of about 5° centigrade below the mean annual temperature of Europe to have all the rigour of the glacial periods back again, or that a rise of 4° to 5° would cause all the Swiss glaciers to disappear. So that one week rather warmer than usual in the Second Interglacial Period would have wrought tremendous damage. The new river-bed would have been torn out to level B, and the first layer of gravel formed by the grinding up of the rocks and flints deposited at C. Then perhaps the winter came on or drier weather. The river shrank, and Abbeville man came down to the water's edge; he wanted to fish or drink; he may have camped there. In any case he left his tools

RIVER TERRACES

behind and these were made of flint, and some are found today nearly as sharp and perfect as when he used them, neither rolled nor abraded. The river rose again, and bringing down more gravel covered up the tools; sometimes it carried an implement along, and bruising it very considerably in so doing deposited it lower down the river.

So man, during all the long years of the Second Interglacial Period, lived on the water's edge of the Somme, and left his tools behind him to be covered up by the gravel deposited in flood times when he had to retreat up to the higher terraces. In the gravels of this terrace are found remains of *Elephas antiquus*, a southern type of elephant which preceded the mammoth. This shows us that the climate was warm.

In the gravels of the first terrace are found later Acheulean implements, but the final gravel bed has not been explored because it is frequently submerged.

It should be noted that disturbances of the level of the earth's surface, in relation to the level of the sea, may have contributed to the formation of river terraces. For instance, well below the bed of the Thames is an old buried channel, in which the river ran when the land was higher. Any raising of the land's surface would make the river run more rapidly on its way to the sea, and so have more power to cut its way down, and form terraces, or it may have been that the Ice Age locked up tremendous quantities of water, and thus lowered the sea-level. Since Neolithic times there has been little change in the earth's surface.

Fig. 5 shows the terraces of the River Wey at Farnham, Surrey, and is included because it is nearer home than the Somme. The gravel beds are shown by solid blacks. At A no implements have been found, so this may have been the bed of an enormous river of pre-glacial times which extended as the dotted line right across the country to Hindhead. The next river formation was on the line B, and of this there are gravel beds remaining on three ridges, valleys between having been cut since to C. D and E show rivers which were gradually shrinking to pygmy dimensions.

It is quite easy to see that such tremendous rivers could not have existed as part of our present river system. The Thames at London meandered over 5 miles, changing course between Highbury and Clapham. Europe in Pleistocene times had a

HOW TO DATE BY GEOLOGY

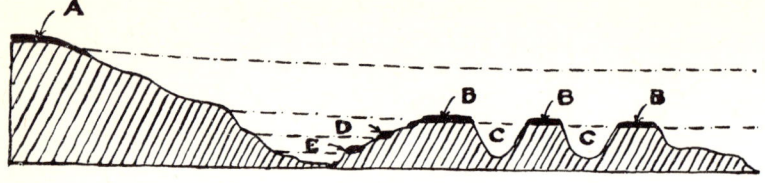

5 The Farnham Terraces

different shape, and was a bigger place than it is now, and raised higher above the sea-level. The Atlantic was perhaps 100 miles more to the west: the Mediterranean consisted of two inland seas.

The Irish Sea, English Channel, and North Sea were wide valleys feeding noble rivers. One had for its tributaries the Thames, Rhine, and Elbe, and it discharged its waters into a northern sea just south of the Faroe Isles. Another, which we will call the River Acheulean Man, had for its tributaries the Seine, Somme, and all our southern rivers, and flowed westward to the Atlantic through the fertile *lands* of what is now the English Channel. England during some parts of the glacial periods was connected to Europe by a watershed of dry land where the Straits of Dover now are. There was an isthmus across the Mediterranean at Gibraltar, and another south of Sicily.

Before we leave the question of rivers and their terraces, we must refer back to fig. *4*. On the upper drawing of the river the gravel of the terraces, which is shown dotted, is overlain by deposits which are shown by hatched lines.

These deposits are in the nature of Loess, or loam. They are what the scientists call sub-aerial deposits, that is, deposited on the surface by the wind, as opposed to sub-aqueous, or under the action of water. The Loess, to which constant reference is made by the archaeologists, is a greyish-brown sandy and chalky loam deposited by wind in the form of dust. This was caused by the action of frost during a glacial period. As the ice retreated the earth would have been a very barren place. There is evidence that at this period there were great winds and blizzards, which swept over these deserts and blew the dust about. This frequently led to the destruction of animal life, and their bones are found now in great quantities embedded in the Loess. The position of

LOESS

the Loess lands is very important; beginning at the Ural Mountains they stretch across South Russia to the Carpathians and the Danube, then by way of the north-west of Austria through South Germany into the north of France. The Loess did not lend itself to the development of thick forest, so this track remained open as a route for prehistoric man from east to west. On the terrace No. 2 of the Somme at St. Acheul(*4*) at its base, on the chalk, are found the gravels with the remains of *E. antiquus*, the southern elephant, and rough flint hand-axes. In the sands over the gravel are more early Abbevillian implements, and these two layers were deposited by water at the same time. Then above this start the sub-aerial deposits. First there is a white sandy loam with land shells. Above this is the older Loess in three layers, consisting of sands, and sandy loams, with gravel at base. Here are found remains of the red deer, and implements of the St. Acheul Period. Above these three layers come three others of the younger Loess, each layer divided by thin sections of gravel, in which are found Moustier implements. Above this comes brick earth, which is weathered Loess, where are found Upper Aurignac and Solutré implements, and in the soil washed down on the extreme top there are implements from the Neolithic to the Iron Age.

Think how bewildering it must have been to find all these evidences of ancient civilization in one and the same terrace, because not only were the implements found in the lowermost gravels of a later age as one went down from terrace 2 to 1, but they also were later in each terrace as one approached the surface.

Out of all these facts, the archaeologists have endeavoured to form a scale of time by which to measure the age of the peoples of the Old Stone Age and their characteristic implements. It seems a splendid picture: all these thousands of years, and man moving through them alert, resourceful, on an upward path!

Chapter II

THE EARLIEST MEN OF THE OLD STONE AGE

WE can now pass to a consideration of the most interesting part of our study—prehistoric man. What did he do on the banks of the Somme, the Thames, or the Wey; how did he fend for himself, his wife, and children? Or did he first look after himself, and preach the doctrine of self-help to the family? Perhaps before we endeavour to sum up his doings, it will be well to take stock of his scanty belongings.

Having done this we shall then have to look about for a model to help us. A painter uses a dummy which he calls a lay-figure; this he dresses up and poses for the picture. In the case of prehistoric man, our model must be drawn from the savage races of modern times; and remember there are still people who use stone because they cannot work iron, but such men are few and far between now, and have lost their old self-reliance and interest by contact with civilization. Obviously we cannot draw any useful comparisons between prehistoric and civilized man; they are poles apart so far as their lives are concerned; but, if we go back a little to the earlier voyagers, we can find records of people who were still living as simple and primitive a life as the prehistoric men.

The first thing to discuss, then, is the stone tools, since these are nearly always the only clues we have to the existence of the earliest men of the Stone Age.

Fig. 6 shows prehistoric man making flint implements. The ones illustrated are about $3\frac{1}{2}$ inches long. The stone held in the right hand acted as a hammer, and with this flakes were knocked off, and shape given to the implement. Flint flaking is an art, as can be easily tested by trying to make an implement oneself. It is a comparatively easy matter to strike off a flake, but a very difficult one to shape it. The actual idea of symmetry marks a great advance, and is the beginning of a sense of proportion; a

FLINT INSTRUMENTS

6 Lower Palaeolithic man makes a flint implement

feeling that the implement will not only cut as well as the rough flake, but that it would look better, and be more pleasant to handle, if it were shaped.

These implements would have had all kinds of uses. Flint can be made as sharp as a razor, and they served as the knives of the day, and were used to cut up a beast, scrape a bone, dig up pignuts, or shape a stick. Flint is extraordinarily hard—until quite

THE EARLIEST MEN OF THE OLD STONE AGE

7 Making fire

recently it was used in connection with steel and tinder to produce fire. If a piece is struck against steel, minute fragments of the latter fly off, heated by the blow to such an extent that they burn in the air as sparks. Prehistoric man probably obtained his fire in this way, using, instead of steel, marcasite, an iron sulphide found in association with flint, or he may have done so by friction, rubbing one piece of wood up and down in a groove in another piece, until the dust ignited (7).

Prehistoric man also used flints fashioned for scraping fat off the skins of the animals he killed, and the bark off all the odd pieces of wood that he must have needed. His spears would have been of wood.

Our readers will, however, agree that the early flints (*10, 11*), the human origin of which is unquestioned, could not have been produced at once. Thousands of years in all probability passed before early man got into his dull head the idea of shape. At first he must have used any stick, stone, or shell that came handy. Probably happy accident came to his aid; he broke a flint and found that it had a keen cutting edge. At the identical moment that it occurred to him to turn this flint into a rough tool by trimming it into shape, he took the first step towards civilizing himself.

When man discovered the use of fire, he had an ally which not only cooked his food and warmed his body, but would at the same time have sharpened and hardened a stick of wood, so that it could be used as a spear. Put any piece of wood in a fire and char the end; when scraped it is pointed in shape.

However, there is no evidence of the use of fire before the late Acheulean, that is to say one of our latest industries in this

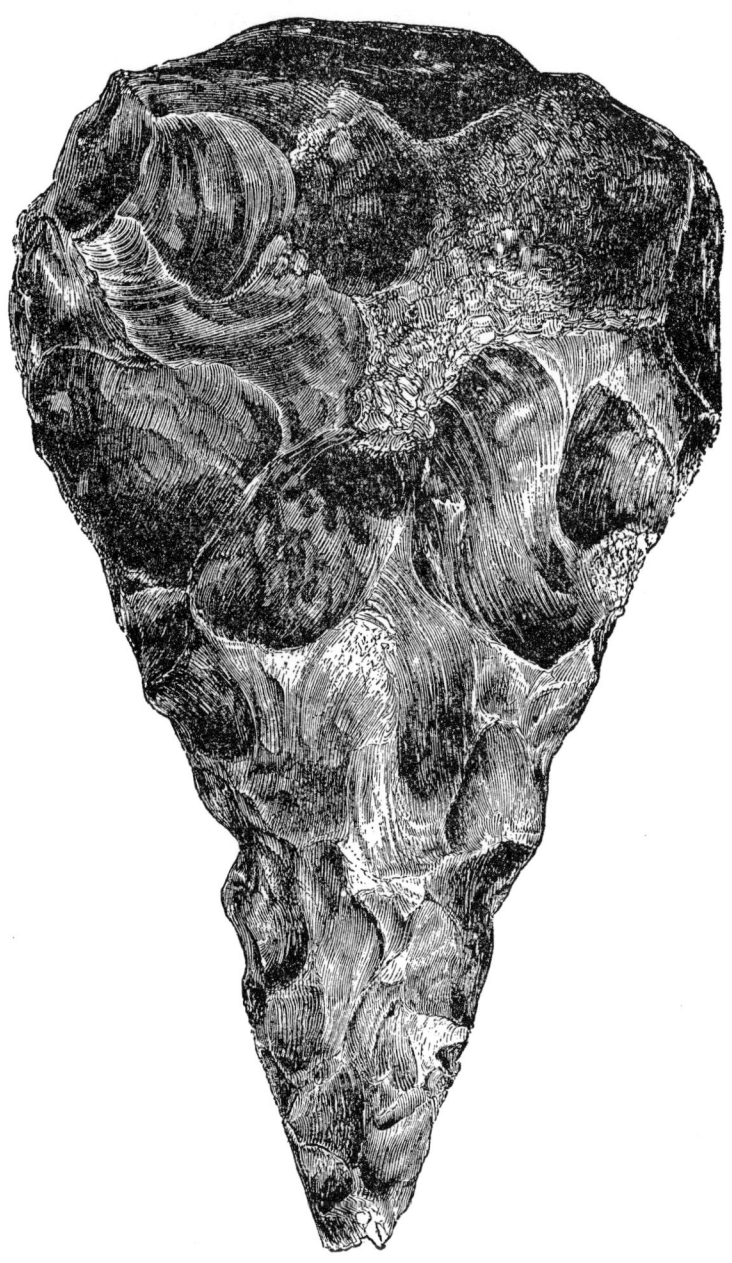

8 Flint implement found near Gray's Inn Lane in the seventeenth century. *After Evans*

THE EARLIEST MEN OF THE OLD STONE AGE

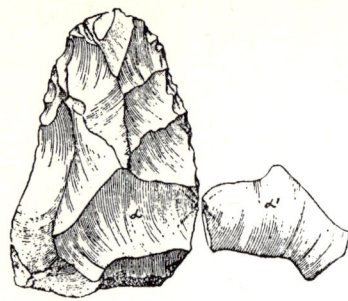

9 How a flake is knocked off a flint hand-axe. *After Oakley*

period, so that it seems that the earliest men must have eaten their animals and vegetables uncooked and to have re-sharpened their wooden spears every time they were used.

The earliest stone tools that we really know anything about are those associated with the second terrace in the Somme Valley, described in our first chapter (*4*) and with other deposits of the same age, in different parts of the world. Some of these tools are very roughly made. There are choppers made by knocking one or two flakes off a river-pebble so as to create a sharp edge, and also tiny flakes three or four inches long. These have been found in the buried channel of the Thames in

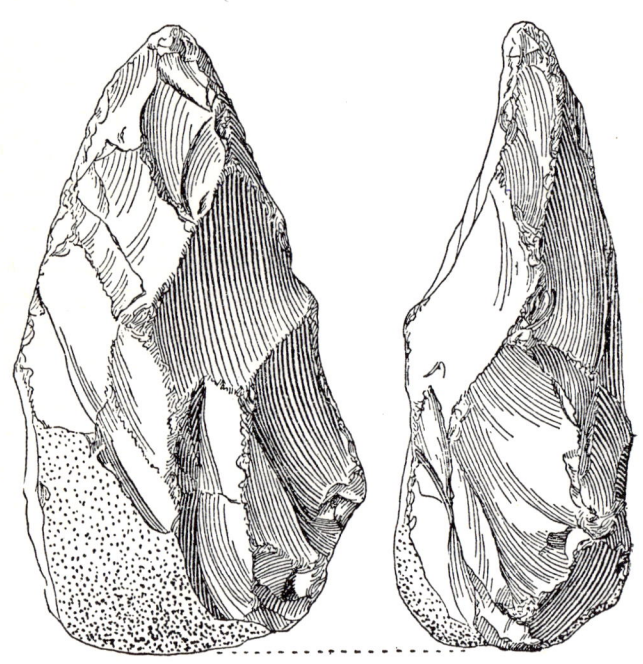

10 Front and side view of an Abbevillian hand-axe

HAND-AXES

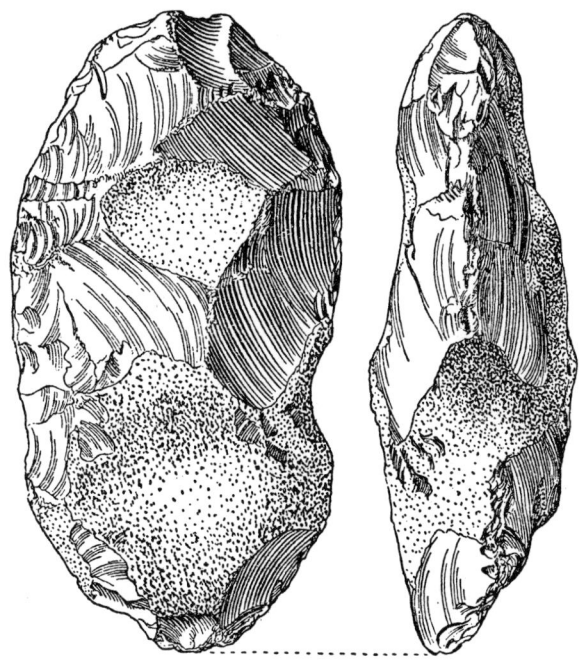

11 Front and side view of an early
(Abbevillian) hand-axe

England, and also in Southern Africa. It is very difficult to believe they have been intentionally made by man, but they occur together in large numbers, in places where man had camped, and together with the more finished tools in the later deposits, so that we must accept them as the earliest tools of all.

However, we are lucky in France and England, for here, in the second terrace of the Somme, and in the Thames terrace of the same age, we have discovered the first easily recognized stone tool, which we call the hand-axe. We illustrate a number of these instruments. The first(8) is one found in Gray's Inn Lane, London, as early as the end of the seventeenth century. It is now in the British Museum. Our beautiful engraving is from an old publication. This is quite a late (Acheulean) hand-axe. For these tools were found to be so useful that they continued to be made for more than 200,000 years, from the Second Interglacial, through the next Glacial and Interglacial Period, right up to the

THE EARLIEST MEN OF THE OLD STONE AGE

beginning of the last glaciation. The earliest hand-axes of the Second Interglacial Period are known as Abbevillian hand-axes, after the site at Abbeville in the Somme Valley. Hand-axes were made by knocking flakes off a pebble or block of flint, or of some other stone if that was not available. They are usually flaked all over except at one end, where the pebble surface is left as a hand-grip. The later, Acheulean, hand-axes, are flaked all over both sides and are much thinner and better made. Fig. *9* shows the Acheulean hand-axe and the flake which has just been knocked off. The reason why the later ones are better made is because Abbevillian man made his hand-axes by hitting them with a harder stone held in the other hand. Acheulean man discovered that if you hit the flint with a rod of wood you had more control and could make a finer flint tool. Figs. *10* and *11* show two Abbevillian hand-axes, figs. *12* and *13* two Acheulean hand-axes. You can see that these later implements are very beautifully made. Yet experiments have shown that they can be made in a minute or two. They also get blunt very easily. At Olorgesailie, in Kenya, an Acheulean camp site has been found hidden under the sand. This is preserved so that you can go there and see the bones of the animals killed by Acheulean man still surrounded by the hand-axes he used to skin and to cut up the meat.

And if you do go there you will see that around the skeleton of one animal there may be more than twenty hand-axes and flakes. All of these have been used to skin and chop up the animal. They were thrown away when they got blunt, or when they broke in half, or just because they were too heavy

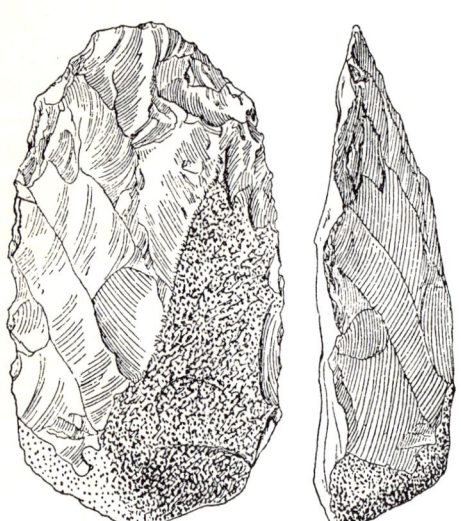

12 Front and side view of an Acheulean hand-axe (Cleaver variety)

HAND-AXES

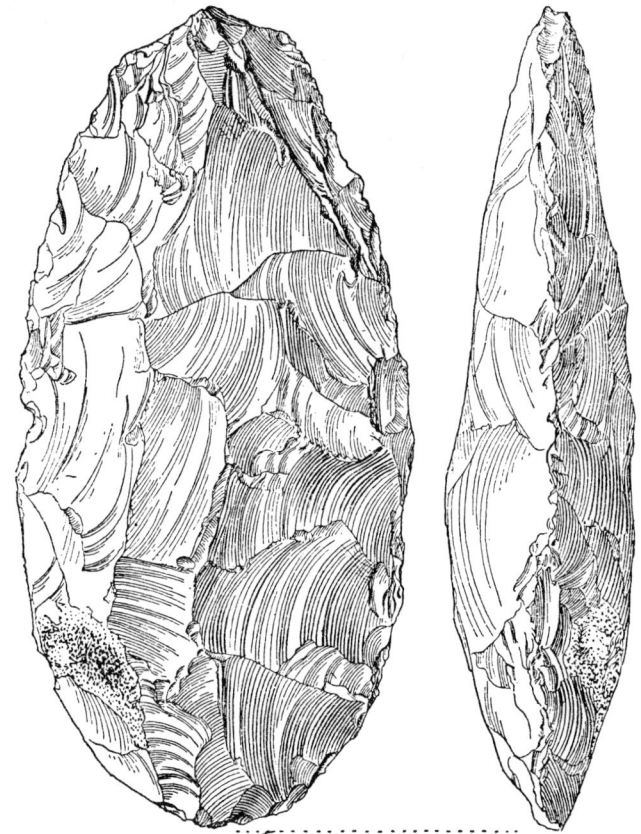

13 Front and side view of an Acheulean hand-axe
(Ovate variety)

to carry away. It was easier to make another hand-axe when it was required.

Many thousands of these flint implements are often found in the same gravel pit and this is thought to prove that large numbers of prehistoric people camped together. This is doubtful; food was scarce. It is, of course, always difficult to remember that an interglacial period extended over tens of thousands of years, so that if a river bank was a favourite camping-place, the tools could have been dropped year after year, and covered up by gravel and sand in times of flood and, if these tools were so

THE EARLIEST MEN OF THE OLD STONE AGE

14   Lower Palaeolithic scraper

easy to make, one man in his life might have made hundreds of them. We dig these implements up today, and forget the long time which it took for the gravel to be deposited. Another point to be borne in mind is that, so far, all the remains of prehistoric man that we have noted have been found near water. The earliest men had to camp by the side of a river, or lake, because they had not any pots or pans in which to store water. Thousands of years passed before man made pottery.

We have said that the earliest hand-axes are those named after Abbeville and the later ones those named after St. Acheul, and in the last chapter we learned how these hand-axes were dated by their position in the gravels of the Somme Valley at these two small French villages. The later hand-axe people, the Acheuleans, also made another sort of tool, a heavy scraper on a large flake and in our illustration you can see a woman using one of these scrapers to cut the marrow she is eating out of a bone.

From their studies archaeologists have discovered that hand-axe man lived in many parts of the world: all over Africa and India, as well as in Western Europe, but in this book we are only going to write about them in England and France. When he lived on the banks of the Somme in France, during the Second Interglacial Period, Abbeville man had as companions two huge elephants, *E. meridionalis* and *E. antiquus*; the hippopotamus, rhinoceros, and sabre-toothed tiger; and a horse, *Equus stenonis*. The naturalists tell us that the teeth of *E. antiquus* were adapted to eating the small branches and foliage of trees. This gives an

EARLY HUNTING

interesting indication of the climate. It must have been warm and genial for these southern animals to have flourished.

How man fended for himself we cannot tell, armed only with a hand-axe which he perhaps hafted as a spear; he could have but little chance against an elephant, 15 feet high to the top of the shoulder.

If looks are any criterion, the sabre-toothed tiger *Machairodus* (*15*) must have been an evil beast. *Machairodus* was widely distributed and existed in England with the cave men who came later on; this we know because his teeth have been found in Kent's Cavern, near Torquay, and Creswell Caves. Man could only have combated such animals by craft; fire and traps were his weapons, and one expects that he was not too proud to eat the remains of the tiger's feast. Fig. *16* is of a pitfall in use today by the natives of British East Africa. To dig the pit would not have been beyond the wit of prehistoric man, and the stakes could have been sharpened and the points hardened by fire. Such a pit would have been a beginning of the long battle between brain and mere bulk. This would have been one way in which prehistoric man obtained the meat that he needed for his food. He was, of course, as carnivorous as his foe the tiger. He possessed neither flocks, nor herds, and did not grow any corn.

Darwin tells us that "the Gaucho in the Pampas, for months together, touches nothing but beef. But they eat, I observed, a very large proportion of fat."

15   *Machairodus*, the Sabre-toothed tiger

THE EARLIEST MEN OF THE OLD STONE AGE

Again, Darwin gives us a splendid picture of how to support life, when there is not a butcher's shop just round the corner, and you have to catch your supper before you can cook it. He was in the Falkland Islands at the time. His Gaucho separated a fat cow from a herd of wild cattle, and caught it with his *lazo*. It was then hamstrung, and killed by driving a knife "into the head of the spinal marrow". A large circular piece of flesh was then cut out of the back, with the skin attached; this was roasted on the embers, with the hide downwards and in the form of a saucer, so that none of the gravy was lost.

Though the weather was wet, the Gauchos managed to light their fire. First with their flint and steel they got a spark on to their piece of charred rag or tinder. Then "they sought beneath the tufts of grass and bushes for a few dry twigs, and these they rubbed into fibres; then surrounding them with coarser twigs, something like a bird's nest, they put the rag with its spark of fire in the middle and covered it up. The nest being then held up to the wind, by degrees it smoked more and more, and at last burst out in flames."

For fuel the Gauchos "found what, to my surprise, made nearly as hot a fire as coals, this was the skeleton of a bullock lately killed, from which the flesh had been picked by the carrion hawks".

16 The pitfall

The huge *Elephas antiquus* remained as a problem for the hunters to tackle. They probably employed the pitfall to trap animals—the Australians still catch emus in this way—or they may have been the inventors of another device which is still employed by native races. This consists of a large and heavy piece of wood, which is suspended above a path,

CLOTHING

pointing downwards, by a grass rope. Fig. *17* shows how the animal, pushing its way along, cracks the rope, with the result that the spear falls on to the spinal column.

We may turn to Darwin to gain information as to the appearance of savage races. Writing of the Fuegians he said: "Their only garment consists of a mantle made of guanaco skin, with the wool outside; this they wear just thrown over their shoulders." But the skin cloak appears to have been a party frock, and not for general use. Darwin saw them in their canoes, the sleet falling and thawing on their naked bodies. He refers to the Fuegian wigwam which "resembles, in size and dimensions, a haycock. It merely consists of a few broken branches stuck in the ground, and very imperfectly thatched on one side with a few tufts of grass and rushes. . . . At Goeree Roads I saw a place where one of these naked men had slept, which absolutely offered no more cover than the form of a hare."

The Tasmanians made much the same form of shelter, using bark instead of grass and rushes, and we have shown the type in fig. *18.* They also went about quite naked, using occasionally a fur cloak. Both the Fuegians and the Tasmanians liberally anointed their bodies and heads with grease mixed with the ochreous earths. In this way they gained a certain protection from the weather, and it helped to keep them clean. Earth is a fine deodorizer.

17 Falling spear

THE EARLIEST MEN OF THE OLD STONE AGE

18   A wind-break

There is a good tale told of a party of Tasmanians given some soup, on the top of which floated fat; this they scooped off with their hands, and put on their heads, but they did not drink the soup. Primitive man almost invariably roasts or bakes his meat.

Later we give instances of human remains being found, buried with red ochre, for use in the spirit world. This points to the covering of grease and ochre having developed from a protection into a decoration of the body.

Darwin wrote of the Fuegians: "The old man had a fillet of white feathers tied round his head, which partly confined his black, coarse, and entangled hair. His face was crossed by two broad transverse bars; one painted bright red, reached from ear to ear and included the upper lip; the other, white like chalk, extended above and parallel to the first, so that even his eyelids were thus coloured."

We have just referred to skeletons being found with colour for decorating the body, and implements for use in the spirit world, and such burials point to a belief in a future life. But we can find no traces as yet of such a belief on the part of the Abbeville man. Captain FitzRoy of the *Beagle* could never ascertain that the Fuegians had any distinct belief in a future

THE MAMMOTH

life. When driven by extreme hunger they killed and ate the old women before their dogs, because, as they said, "Doggies catch otters, old women no".

We have described the sub-aerial deposits on the terraces of the Somme (p. 32). It should be noted that the earliest St. Acheul types are found in the sands and gravels at the base of the older Loess, and the later types in the upper strata. This older Loess is in three layers. It is supposed to have been deposited in glacial times; it seems as if the weather gradually became colder. This view is borne out by the remains of the animals found and in the implements. In the sand and gravel of the earlier St. Acheul times at the base of the older Loess, we have our old friend *E. antiquus* and the red deer, both southern animals; but in the older Loess itself, we meet for the first time *E. primigenius* (the mammoth), *Rhinoceros tichorhinus* (the woolly-coated one), horse, and lion. These were northern animals who came south as the weather became colder and the Fourth Glacial Period drew on.

The mammoth was not so large as *E. antiquus*, and closely resembled the existing Indian elephant, excepting only the tusks, which were very long and curved. Its teeth were more adapted for eating coarse grasses than the foliage of trees. The country was becoming barer and bleaker, and trees were scarce. Its

19   *Elephas primigenius*, the mammoth

THE EARLIEST MEN OF THE OLD STONE AGE

20 *Rhinoceros tichorhinus*, the woolly-coated Rhinoceros

curved tusks perhaps acted as hay-rakes, and helped to gather up food. Its warm coat and thick skin, with a layer of fat under, protected it from the cold weather. We know all about the mammoth, because whole carcases have been dug up in the frozen Arctic regions, with the flesh, skin, and furry coats, protected through the ages by the ice and snow in which they were embedded. Fig. *19* gives a general idea of this animal, and fig. *20* shows the woolly-coated rhinoceros.

It will be seen that during St. Acheul times the weather in England and France was getting colder, and as the ice-cap crept down, so these animals from the northern regions retreated before it. Man for the same reason appears to have looked about for warmer shelter than the open-air camps, and to have retreated to the caves and caverns.

Now that we have learned something about Abbeville and St. Acheul man, it would be nice to be able to say something about what he looked like. Unfortunately very few fossil human bones have been found belonging to this period. In 1891 Professor E. Dubois found the roof of a skull, two molar teeth, and a thigh-bone (femur) on the banks of the River Solo, at Trinil in Java. The position is interesting because of its relation to Australia and Tasmania. The remains were discovered in river deposit of late Pliocene, or early Pleistocene, character, and were found in conjunction with the bones of many of the lower animals of the same period; but there were no implements.

The brain-pan of Pithecanthropus exceeds that of any ape, and equals about two-thirds that of modern man. The man was long-headed or dolichocephalic. Professor G. Elliot Smith thinks that its features prove that the man belonged to the human family, and enjoyed rudimentary powers of speech. Darwin, writing of the Fuegians, said: "The language of those

THE JAVA APE-MAN

people, according to our notions, scarcely deserves to be called articulate. Captain Cook has compared it to a man clearing his throat, but certainly no European ever cleared his throat with so many hoarse, guttural, and clicking sounds." The thighbone of Pithecanthropus shows that he walked upright, but the teeth are more simian than human. Pithecanthropus was a link between gibbon and man. He probably retreated to the trees when he was alarmed, and may have contrived rough shelters or nests there, but of this, of course, we cannot be sure. The scientists went to Java because Europe was deserted by the manlike apes in early Pliocene times, when the temperature became colder. A more genial climate than ours was necessary for the development of this link which, with brain, added to bone and muscle, was to connect them with us.

21 Pithecanthropus—The Java Ape-Man

It is sad that Professor Dubois could not find any tools or implements associated with Pithecanthropus.

The skull itself is what the scientists call mesaticephalic in shape, cephalic index about 78, and, as we shall be constantly meeting this and other terms used in relation to skulls, we will explain them now. The cephalic index is the ratio or percentage of the breadth of the head to the length, the latter being taken as 100.

Skulls with index of 70–75 = Dolichocephalic (long).
,,   ,,   ,, 75–80 = Mesaticephalic (intermediate).
,,   ,,   ,, 80–85 = Brachycephalic (short).

For example, assuming a skull has a breadth of 135 millimetres and a length of 180, we get $\frac{135 \times 100}{180}$ = cephalic index of 75.

THE EARLIEST MEN OF THE OLD STONE AGE

A few teeth and pieces of skull-bone belonging to Pithecanthropus have also been found in China, but this man does not seem to have used hand-axes, though he belongs to the same period as these tools. The only remains of hand-axe man that we know are those found at Heidelberg in Germany and at Swanscombe in Kent.

Of the former only the jaw was found, 80 feet deep in a sand pit at Mauer, near Heidelberg. The jaw gives an impression of enormous strength, and juts out like the ram of a battleship, without any concavity to form a chin. The teeth are human, without projecting canines.

At Swanscombe in Kent gravel from an old river terrace is worked for building and other purposes. At various times implements identical with those found at St. Acheul have turned up in the Middle Gravel (layer) and it was watched with an eagle eye by an antiquary, Mr. A. T. Marston, as the workmen daily exposed more and more of that promising seam. It was not implements he hoped for, but fossil man. In June 1935 he was rewarded by a fragment of the back of a skull. If only another fragment could be found to give a missing clue! And it was, in March 1936—part of the same skull. It can be dated with certainty to St. Acheul times and, most important, represents a type very like modern man. It is most surprising that he antedates by many thousands of years the more simian and wholly different Neanderthal man of the Mousterian period, whose acquaintance we shall make in the next chapter.

Before we pass on to the Cave-dwellers, let us sum up what we have found out about prehistoric man, and draw some comparisons. We say that he was a nomad and a hunter, but unless we are careful to think a little, the mental picture we form is of someone rather like ourselves; a little rougher perhaps, and more whiskery, but with a background of solid comfort somewhere. We shall be right in imagining the man with an active brain, but comfort as we understand it did not exist for him.

We do not realize that prehistoric man was a nomad, or wanderer, because he had to hunt for his food; that unless he hunted he starved. It is really extremely difficult to imagine a state of affairs when a man's sole possessions consisted of a flint hand-axe for tool; a wooden spear for a weapon, and a skin for covering; when all else had to be sought; when pots and pans

LIFE IN THE EARLIEST TIMES

did not exist; when pottery and weaving had not been invented. Yet such people have existed until comparatively recent times. Tasmania was discovered in 1642, by Abel Janszoon Tasman, who named it Van Diemen's Land, after Anthony Van Diemen, the Governor of the Dutch East Indies. It has been renamed after its discoverer. After his time Tasmania was visited by other voyagers, Captain Cook being one in 1777, and they found the Tasmanians to be to all intents and purposes a palaeolithic people. It seems as if, in remote ages, when Asia, like Europe, had a different coast-line, the Tasmanians had come from the mainland into Australia and, retreating again before stronger races, found their way in the end into Tasmania, before it was so much cut off as it is now. There may have been an isthmus across Bass Strait, as there was in Europe across the Straits of Dover. At some later period this disappeared, and the Tasmanians were left free to remain the simple primitive folk they were when first discovered.

They had not the use of iron, and their only tools were made of flint, and very rough ones at that. Generally the Tasmanians went about quite naked, but on occasions wore a skin cloak. Kangaroo skins were dressed as rugs to sit upon. Wet and cold did not appear to harm them, and their houses (*18*) were the merest wind-breaks. When in 1831 the miserable remainder of the natives were exiled to Flinders Island, and lodged in huts, it was found that they caught cold far more readily than when living in the open. Like the Fuegians in their native state, they greased their bodies, and anointed themselves with red ochre; this gave a certain protection. They were also fond of making necklaces of shells, and ornamented their bodies by forming patterns of scars (cicatrization) left by cuts made with a sharp flint. They were nomads moving about the country in search of food; this meant that in hard times the very old and infirm people were left to die, and sometimes the babies had to be sacrificed.

In hunting game like kangaroo they used plain spears made of a hard wood. This is not quite the simple thing it seems. Pithecanthropus would have picked up any long stick to hit with, and it may have slipped from his hand. He then discovered that unless one end was heavier than the other, it did not follow a very straight line of flight; it might knock down a bird, but

THE EARLIEST MEN OF THE OLD STONE AGE

would not pierce with its point the skin of an animal. So through the long ages the Tasmanian spear developed. This was cut, trimmed, and scraped with flint. The end was charred by fire, and so hardened, and then pointed by scraping. The point was at the heavy end; 20 inches from this the circumference was 3 inches, in the middle $2\frac{1}{4}$ inches, and 2 inches from the end only $\frac{1}{2}$ inch. The total length was 11 feet 11 inches. The Tasmanian could throw this and kill an animal at from 40 to 50 yards, and did not use a throwing-stick, as fig. *27*. Unlike the Australians they used neither boomerangs nor shields. Their other weapon was the waddy, or wooden club, about 2 feet 6 inches long, and they threw stones with great accuracy.

The Tasmanian wooden spear had its counterpart in England in the Old Stone Age. It is apparently the broken head, about 15 inches long, of a wooden spear, pointed at one end, and about $1\frac{1}{2}$ inch diameter at the other. It looks exactly as if the end had been broken off the Tasmanian spear and was found at Clacton in Essex, in the *E. antiquus* bed in association with an early type of flint implement. This spear-head is now exhibited in the Natural History Museum at South Kensington.

The Tasmanians were wonderful trackers, with very acute sight, hearing, and smell. They ate the animals and birds they caught. Without any preliminaries these were thrown on to a wood fire which singed the hair and feathers and half-cooked the carcase. Then the bodies were cut apart with a flint and gutted, and the cooking finished off by spitting the joints on sticks, and toasting over the fire. A little wood ash served instead of salt. The meat was always roasted, because there were not any pots to boil it in.

The Tasmanians ate shell-fish as well, and these the women caught by diving into the sea and searching the rocks under water. They did not have nets, hooks, or lines. The women were not treated very well, and had to do all the other work while the men hunted. They sat behind their lords at meals, who, reclining on one arm in Roman fashion, passed the tougher morsels to their dutiful spouses.

The Tasmanians had one notable possession: their raft. This was not hollow like a boat, but made of cigar-shaped rolls of very light bark like cork. One large central roll had two smaller ones lashed to it with grass rope to prevent rolling (see section

THE TASMANIANS

on fig. *22*), so that it was a raft in canoe shape. With these, or in them, they crossed from headland to headland, and the type may have been a survival of the earlier boats by which their ancestors found their way down from the mainland, and bridged the gaps between the islands, if the isthmus we referred to on p. 51 did not exist.

This raft is of great interest, because at some time or other it must have been a notable development. Pithecanthropus, if he ever went boating, did so on any floating log, and discovered to his disgust that it needed pointing, if it was to be paddled along, and also that some sort of arrangement was necessary to prevent it rolling over in the water, and giving him an involuntary bath. The beginning came in some such way. One development was the dug-out, and certain prehistoric men, with fire and flint, shaped and hollowed their log in this way.

The Tasmanian was another and very much readier method. The rafts were used for fishing, and carried three or four men comfortably; the spear, which was their only fishing implement, served as well for a pole. A clay floor was made at one end, and here a fire was lighted.

It is difficult for us to realize, with matches at hand, what a

22 A bark raft

THE EARLIEST MEN OF THE OLD STONE AGE

23 Making grass rope

precious possession fire was to any primitive people. To obtain it they had to follow the method Darwin saw practised by the Tahitians. "A light was procured by rubbing a blunt-pointed stick in a groove made in another, as if with the intention of deepening it, until by friction the dust became ignited"(7). It must have been a difficult business, depending on a supply of dry moss, or fibrous bark, which could be lighted from the dust set on fire by friction. The Tasmanian then carried his fire about with him in the form of decayed touchwood, which would smoulder for hours, and could then be blown into flame.

They made grass rope and string, by twisting long wiry grass or fibrous bark(23). This illustration is of interest, in that it leads up to the development of the spinning spindle shown in fig. 33. Primitive man, of course, used sinews and hide thongs for ties. They also made clumsy reed baskets. With a grass rope they climbed high trees. They passed the rope round themselves and the tree; cut holes in the bark for their big toes, first on one side, and then the other, and as they went up, jerked the rope and themselves up the tree together.

It is not known if they had any idea of trade or barter, but they did not grow any crops, or possess any domesticated animals.

If they ailed, an incision was made in the body, to let the pain escape. The dead were sometimes burned, and sometimes placed in hollow trees. After burning, the remains might be buried, but the skull retained and worn as a memento, or at other times this was buried separately. They believed in a life after death on a pleasant island with their ancestors.

We will finish off this account of the Tasmanians by an amusing description of one of the ways they had of settling their quarrels: "The parties approach one another face to face, and folding their arms across their breasts, shake their heads (which occasionally come in contact) in each other's faces, uttering at

LIFE IN ACHEULEAN TIMES

the same time the most vociferous and angry expressions, until one or the other is exhausted, or his feelings of anger subside." An extremely sensible method, and amusing for the onlookers, which is more than can be said of civilized methods of quarrelling.

It is not very creditable to the civilized white races that the Tasmanians should have been used so badly that they have now become extinct. Truganini, the last survivor, died in 1877, and, we hope, found the dream of the pleasant island and the kindly ancestors come true. A nation can die of a broken heart, even as individuals; or shall we say, they lose heart. Think of a people who have supported life with no other aid than spears, waddies, and chipped flints, then other people come in ships, with a wonderful apparatus for living, which makes the sticks and stones seem foolish and inadequate. Thus the old people lose interest, and heart, and the desire to go on living, or become hangers-on, and so come to an end.

We have written enough to prove that Abbeville and Acheul men, in their flint hand-axes, possessed tools with which they could make the spears that they needed to kill game for food; their mode of living must have been very similar to the Tasmanians. Let us now try to conjure up a picture of a tribe here in England in Abbeville and Acheul times, and find out if we can how they supported life.

The tribe was like a large family in those days. There might have been a headman, who would have been the boldest of the hunters, but little if any system of government. The women did all the work, and looked after the children, and meant more to them than the father, whose place was with the hunters. So much was this the case that the custom grew up in savage races of tracing descent on the mother's side.

The tribe would not have been particularly quarrelsome, unless their neighbours trespassed on their hunting-grounds. War is a civilized institution, based as a rule on the desire to obtain some other nation's property. Prehistoric man had little temptation in this way. Our tribe may have camped on the banks of the Wey for the summer. The river was a much bigger one than it is now, and they possibly found the fishing good. In any case they would only have had the wooden spear to lance

THE EARLIEST MEN OF THE OLD STONE AGE

the fish, and a flint hand-axe to cut it up afterwards. There would have been berries to eat, the roots of bracken and ferns, and nuts in the autumn, crab apples, wild cherries, and sloes. The bee had to give up his store to greedy hands that tore the comb, and crunched it up without waiting to run out the honey. There were snails and shell-fish, grubs and beetles, and luscious caterpillars.

Greatest joy of all, in the earlier age of different climatic conditions, a dead elephant, or hippo, or perhaps a rhinoceros; then would the tribe have sat down, and eaten their way through the carcase.

But rough plenty would not last; hard times and winter would come on, and the tribe range far and wide in search of food. They would grow lean-ribbed as wolves, and just as savage. They would be driven by hunger to attack living game, and in the fight some would die that the others might live. The survivors at the meal would not have presented a pleasant spectacle; they would have torn the beast to pieces, and eaten it raw.

Chapter III

THE FIRST CAVE-DWELLERS

OUR next period is that of the Cave-dwellers, or Moustier men, so called after the cave of Le Moustier, in the valley of the Vézère, Dordogne. At Le Moustier the river has in course of time cut its way down through the limestone, which is left in cliff formation at the sides. In cliffs, caverns were formed by surface water finding its way down from the top through vertical joints and dissolving the rock, or by the river cutting out holes in the banks. This left the caves ready for the occupation of man, and, as the weather became colder, he looked about and found ready-made houses, a thing we should like to do today. When prehistoric man first inhabited these, they were just above the flood-level of the river; today they are often high up on the banks, because the river has continued to cut out its bed. All along the Vézère are caves, which are known all the world over by archaeologists, and later on we shall hear of La Madeleine, La Micoque, Crô-Magnon, and others.

We will start by considering Moustier man. In 1907 a skeleton was discovered in a cave on the banks of the Sourdoire, a tributary of the Dordogne, in the district of La Chapelle-aux-Saints. Let us at once point out that this is the first time we have found any evidence of people burying their dead in a place of sepulchre. The man of Java, and the man of Heidelberg, just dropped in their tracks, were brought down by the river currents, settled into the mud, and were covered up by gravel. In the case of the man of La Chapelle-aux-Saints, it is evident that he had been buried with care and perhaps love. Flint implements were laid ready to his hand for use in the hunting-grounds of the spirit world, and food for his sustenance. Think of the difference this means in the mental outlook of the relatives, and regard it as a notable step up the ladder of civilization. A similar discovery was also made at Le Moustier in 1909.

These discoveries were very important, because they enabled

24 Moustier cave-dwellers

NEANDERTHAL MAN

the archaeologists to be quite sure of their facts in respect to other skeletons which had been found. In 1856 a specimen was discovered in a limestone cave in Neanderthal, near Düsseldorf, Germany; unfortunately, the workmen who found it, not realizing its value, damaged it badly. Remember the Java man was not discovered until 1891, so the scientists were not prepared for the Neanderthaler in 1856. Some said the latter individual must have suffered from "something on the brain", to have had such an extraordinary shape to his head, but Huxley the great Englishman and others recognized the skull as human. From time to time various other skulls were found, until that of La Chapelle-aux-Saints confirmed the opinion that all belonged to one race, which is called the Neanderthal man (*Homo Neanderthalensis*).

The most noticeable characteristic of the Moustier skull is the one very prominent ridge going right across the brows. The frontal bones are very thick, and there is not much chin to the lower jaw. The head is large in proportion to the height. The brain of the La Chapelle-aux-Saints man had a capacity of 1620 c.c., which is about the average modern European capacity of 1550 c.c.; but in brains it is quality, not quantity, which counts. The shin and thigh bones suggest that the man stood with knees bent forward a little. The arm, again, is longer than that of modern man. It should be noticed that the head is placed on the shoulders in quite a different way from ours. If any of our readers stand with bent knees, they will find that the head and shoulders swing forward. Moustier man must have loped along, head to ground like a hunting animal, and would have found it difficult to look up.

Moustier man was widely distributed, and though he seems to have been the first to use the cave, he did not entirely desert the camping-places of his ancestors on the river banks. He is supposed to have lived at the end of the Fourth Glacial Period, so perhaps, as the weather gradually became warmer, he spent some of his summers on the Somme.

25 Poise of the Neanderthal figure

THE FIRST CAVE-DWELLERS

Here M. Commont has identified his implements in the Ergeron, or younger Loess, which, as we have seen (p. 32), was deposited by wind on the terraces.

We had our own cave-dwellers here in England, and Kent's Cavern, one mile to the east of Torquay harbour, Devon, is well worth visiting, because it was one of their homes. Here in the water-worn passages cut out in the limestone hill, we shall find ample evidence of the occupation of man. The excavators found first a black mould deposited in historic times, then a floor of stalagmite in places 3 feet thick. Under this, reddish cave-earth, with bones of the mammoth, rhinoceros, elk, hyena, cave bear, and sabre-toothed tiger, and traces of the fires of prehistoric man.

Under the cave-earth is another floor of stalagmite, and under this again a natural concrete called breccia, in which were found the bones of the cave bear, and flint implements rougher than those discovered in the cave-earth.

The hand-axe disappeared soon after the beginning of the Moustier period; this in St. Acheul times was made by knocking flakes off a nodule of flint. The flakes were used for making small scrapers and the like. Moustier man appears to have dressed one side of his implement first on the nodule, and then to have detached it as a large flake. This, again, is an interesting fact, and shows that man was beginning to economize in the use of material. The weather, too, was becoming colder, and the hills would have been covered with snow. Flint is only found in chalk of the Cretaceous beds. In many parts of the country it has all been cut away by the action of water, and the flints taken with it to form gravel in the river terraces lower down. Flint suitable for making implements must have been valuable to prehistoric man, and a stray flint from the surface is not so good for flaking as one quarried out of chalk exposures. So for some it meant a long journey, and encounters with woolly rhinoceros *en route*, to obtain the raw material for their industry, then perhaps the bartering of skins in exchange for the flints, and a toilsome carrying home of the heavy stones. Perhaps it occurred to Moustier man that if instead of wasting a whole large flint to make one hand-axe, he used the flakes, he could make several implements out of one nodule. This is what he did, and it marks one more step up the ladder.

THE BOLAS

Levallois flakes, also used by Moustier man, are a peculiar type struck from a prepared "tortoise" core, so that the flake has a faceted butt. Sharp-pointed flints are also found notched on one side, evidently for use as spear-heads (26).

Spherical balls of limestone have been found, and it is thought that these may have been used as bolas. Darwin describes the bolas used by the Gauchos of Monte Video, South America. "The bolas, or balls, are of two kinds. The simplest, which is chiefly used for catching ostriches, consists of two round stones covered with leather, and united by a thin plaited thong about 8 feet long; the other kind differs only in having three balls united by thongs to a common centre. The Gaucho holds the smallest of the three in his hand, and whirls the other two round and round his head; then, taking aim, sends them like chain shot revolving through the air. The balls no sooner strike any object than, winding round it, they cross each other and become firmly hitched." The Gaucho lives on horseback, but the Eskimo goes on foot, and he uses a bolas with seven or eight cords, and attached stones, and this he uses to bring down birds on the wing. The stones are formed by being knocked together till they become round.

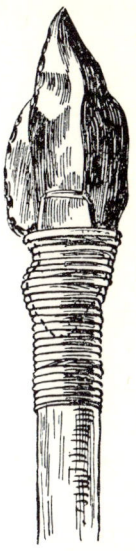

26   Moustier spear-head

The Reindeer and Musk Ox were new-comers from the north in Moustier times, and were hunted by prehistoric man for his food; but we do not find anything that would lead us to suppose that he had as yet domesticated animals.

There is one very black mark against the Moustier people, and that is evidence which is supposed to point to cannibalism, contained in deposits in the Rock Shelter of Krapina, in Croatia. Here were found human bones which had been broken, as if to extract the marrow, and burnt by fire. We shall find on p. 67 that the Australian aborigines, while not being habitual cannibals, yet practised this dreadful habit, as a ceremonial way of disposing of the dead bodies of their relatives.

It will be seen from the foregoing that, though we know a little more about the Moustier men than about those of Chelles and St. Acheul, it does not amount to very much. We must then

THE FIRST CAVE-DWELLERS

27 Australian spear-throwing

search for some primitive people living under similar conditions, and at about the same stage of civilization as that of Moustier, and see if we can draw useful comparisons. The aborigines of Australia are such a people. Of them Messrs. Spencer and Gillen have written that they "have no idea of permanent abodes, no clothing, no knowledge of any implements save those fashioned out of wood, bone, and stone, no idea whatever of the cultivation of crops, or of the laying in of a supply of food to tide over hard times, no word for any number beyond three, and no belief in anything like a supreme being". They have not been treated quite so brutally as were the Tasmanians, and are still allowed to exist on sufferance, and end their days as a race on the unfertile lands. In the beginning, it seems as if they followed the Tasmanians into Australia from the mainland, and settled there, driving some of the latter people into Tasmania.

The Australian Aborigines' spear shows a considerable development on that of the Tasmanians, and may possibly resemble that used by the Moustier man. About 10 feet long, some have hardwood points on to which barbs were spliced. Others have a flint point(*26*). The Australians use a spear-thrower. This has many forms, but the essential feature is a stick about a yard long, with a handle at one end, and a peg at the other. Figs. *27* and *28* show the spear-thrower in use. First the end of the spear is fitted on to the peg of the thrower. This is held in the right hand well behind the body, the left hand

THE AUSTRALIAN ABORIGINES

balancing the spear. It is then thrown up and forward, the thrower imparting an additional impulse as the spear leaves the hand. Darwin when in Australia saw the natives at practice. He wrote: "A cap being fixed at thirty yards distance, they transfixed it with a spear, delivered by the throwing-stick with the rapidity of an arrow from the bow of a practised archer."

This short range means that the Australian must be an expert hunter and tracker, if he is to approach within striking distance of his quarry, the kangaroo. Moustier spear-throwers have not been discovered in Europe as yet, but we can safely assume that the shorter type was not arrived at without many simpler forms going before. The Australian uses a wooden shield, which is a development on the Tasmanian equipment. Very much narrower than those of mediaeval times, it is a long oval in shape, varying from 2 feet to 2 feet 6 inches in length, by 6 to 12 inches in width. Rounded on the outside, the inside of the shield is hollowed out so as to leave a vertical handle. When one thinks that this is all cut out of the solid with a flint, it becomes a notable piece of work. The shield points to quarrels and fighting, because its only purpose can be to protect the user against spear thrusts. We do not know if the Moustier men used shields.

Our readers should pay a visit to the Ethnographical Gallery at the British Museum, and see there a spear-head made by an Australian in recent times, from broken bottle-glass; it is an

28   Australian spear-throwing

THE FIRST CAVE-DWELLERS

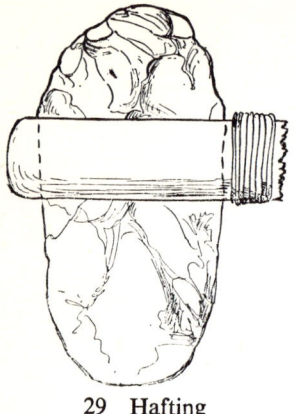

29 Hafting

astonishing production, and the man who made it a great craftsman. A visit should also be paid to the Stone Age Room where there are Moustier types, and so comparisons can be drawn.

The Australians make very useful knives out of long dagger-shaped flakes of stone, and by daubing resin at one end form rounded handles. They mount sharp flakes in the ends of sticks with resin, and these are used as chisels and adzes. There are stone picks inserted like the spear-heads in cleft sticks, only at right angles; these were secured with tendons and resin. Stone axes are made, and these are hafted in a withy handle, made supple by heat, and then bent around the axe, and fastened with tendons and resin.

Some of the Australian implements in the British Museum are ground and polished, and here in Europe we associate this with the next period, the Neolithic. The methods of hafting are of great interest, and prehistoric people must also have used some such way to protect their hands from the razor-like edges

30 Australian hut

CLOTHING AND ORNAMENT

of the flints. Like the Tasmanians, the Australians walk abroad without any clothes, but wear skin cloaks in their huts; they stitch these together with sinew, and use bone awls and pins for piercing the skins. Necklaces and forehead bands of shells and teeth are worn, and they make themselves beautiful by pushing a short stick, called a

31   Making fire

nosepin, through the thin membrane which divides the nostrils. Their bodies are anointed with grease and red ochre. They also sacrifice joints of their little fingers, as we shall find the Aurignac men did in Europe. Their huts are very simple, and serve for the camp of a day or so, which makes a break in their wanderings. Fig. *30* shows such a type, which may have been used by Moustier man in the summer when he left his cave. It represents the next development that we should expect from the Tasmanian's wind-break (*18*). It is, in fact, like two wind-breaks leaning together, and was made of any rough branches that came to hand.

The Australians have another method of lighting fires by friction: one stick is held in the hands and rotated in a hole in another, until the wood dust is ignited (*31*). Darwin gives an improvement on this method: "the Gaucho in the Pampas . . . taking a pliant stick about 18 inches long, presses one end on his breast, and the other pointed end into a hole in a piece of wood, then rapidly turns the curved part like a carpenter's centre-bit".

Another interesting development is the bark canoe of the Australians (*32*). The lines of this are much the same as that of the Tasmanians (*22*), but the construction is that of a real boat, not a raft. A long strip of bark is stripped from the gum tree with a stone axe and warmed over a fire to make it supple. Curved saplings, bent as ribs, give the shape, and a stretcher goes across the tops of these, and the boat is prevented from spreading by grass rope ties from side to side. The prow and stern are tied up with stringy bark. A small fire is carried on a

THE FIRST CAVE-DWELLERS

clay floor. The Australians are great fishermen, and have invented a barbed harpoon, and fish-hooks of shell and wood.

The point of the comparison is that in Europe, after Moustier times, we come across well-made harpoons, which could only have been used for fishing. These could not have developed without long experiment. Moustier man may have gone fishing with a spear without barbs, and from his poor catches may have thought out the more effective harpoon. Therefore they must have used some form of canoe, which, of course, has long since disappeared, so we turn to another primitive people for inspiration. The Australians make another form of canoe where bark is sewn on to the framework. The coracle of Wales and Ireland, the kayak and umiak of the Eskimo, were of this form, only skins were used instead of bark, and this may have been the Moustier method. We do know that in Europe in Neolithic times the dug-out canoe was employed.

The Australians carry on trade by barter. The red ochre they need for decorating their bodies, may be exchanged for stone suitable for making implements. They have not any form of writing, but send news about by message-sticks. There is one in the British Museum from North Queensland. It resembles a short wooden lath about 3 inches long, with zigzag cuts and

32   A bark canoe

FOOD GATHERING

notches. The meaning of the message is "that the dogs are being properly cared for, and that the writer wants clothes". The lady would not have worn more than a skin cloak, with perhaps a hair fringe round her waist, and a necklace of shells, so that her dress allowance would not have needed to have been a very large one. The Australians are excellent hunters, as were the Tasmanians. Kangaroos are eaten, also almost all the other animals and birds, grubs and the pupæ of ants, fish and shellfish. Their cooking is very much like that of the Tasmanians (p. 52), the animals being first gutted are cooked in a pit. All tendons are removed for use.

Another notable development is that the women collect the seeds of various grasses and plants, and grind these down between stones and winnow by pouring from one *pitchi* into another, so that the husks are blown away. They make rough cakes of the resulting flour. The *pitchi* is a shallow wooden trough used for shovel or scoop as well. The Moustier men may have collected seeds in the same way, and so have started the long chain which led up to the household loaf of today. The Australian women use a yam or digging-stick, like the one illustrated (*60*), but not loaded with a stone to increase weight. The yam-stick is not used to cultivate the soil, but for digging up honey ants or lizards which are eaten. Remember we have seen that Darwin found people living exclusively on meat, and that this was general before the advent of agriculture; but this collecting of seeds would naturally have suggested the idea of growing plants for food.

The Australians did not practise cannibalism, except in a ceremonial way, when, as is the case in Victoria, they regarded it as a reverent method of disposing of dead relatives.

We have seen (p. 54) that the Tasmanians made rush baskets, and grass rope for climbing trees and tying up their rafts. With the rope they would have learned the principle of twisting together short lengths of fibre, so that these made a continuous string. This is the principle of all spinning. The Arunta tribes in Central Australia can manufacture twine of fur or human hair. For this they use a spindle (*33*, A): this is a stick about 14 inches long, which at the spinning end is pushed through holes in two thin, curved sticks, about 6 inches long, placed at right angles to

THE FIRST CAVE-DWELLERS

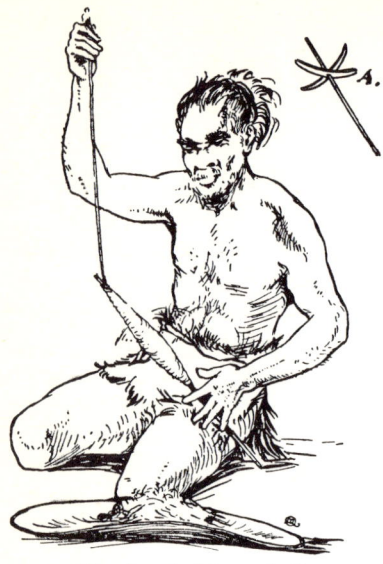

33   A primitive spindle

one another. Some fur or hair is pulled out, and part of it twisted with the finger into a thread long enough to be tied on to the end of the spindle; this is rotated by being rubbed up or down the thigh. The remainder of the fur held in the hand is allowed to be drawn out as the spindle twists the thread; this is then wound up on to the spindle, and more of the fur paid out, and more thread twisted. This, we think, is the greatest achievement of the Australians, and they, as we have seen, are to all intents and purposes living in a Stone Age. The problem is, for how long they have used the spindle; did they bring it with them in remote ages from the mainland; did prehistoric man, whom the Australians so closely resemble, use a spindle? They must have needed rope, and if they made it in this way, then the sixteenth-century spinning-wheel, and the eighteenth-century spinning-jenny, would have their roots very deep in the past, because both are only mechanically driven spindles which trace their descent from something like fig. *33*. The Australian does not use his twine for weaving, but contents himself with making net bags. Fig. *23* shows a still more primitive method of making twine out of long shreds of bark.

The Australians have a very complicated system of relationship. A group will be divided into two classes or phratries: one-half may be Crows, the other Lizards. A Crow would marry a Lizard, not another Crow; would be kind to all the other Crows, and regard the birds of that name as feathered friends. This was a means not only of binding men together in fellowship and friendship, but of preserving the decencies, and preventing the marriage of persons too closely related for it to be seemly. Each group had various ceremonies, generally concerned with invoking the totem animal to promote plenty. In Aurignac times

RELATIVES AND SOCIETY

in Europe, it is suggested that the cave paintings may have had totemic significance. Totemism is very widely spread, and gives us a new respect for primitive peoples; it shows them shaping their lives to a system, and not just chattering their way along like so many monkeys.

The Australians have not any other settled form of government, but each group or tribe has a headman, who by reason of skill in hunting or special gifts takes the lead. They are not a quarrelsome people. War is a terrible luxury in which primitive man cannot afford to indulge. His quarrels are mere skirmishes as to boundaries of hunting-grounds; it never occurs to the Australian to steal his neighbour's territory. In his opinion this is inhabited by the spirits of their ancestors, and so would be a useless possession to him.

The Australians very frequently associate death not with natural causes, but with magic wrought by an enemy. This leads to trouble, because if the medicine man of the tribe names the enemy, and the enemy is a neighbour, he is tracked down and put to death. In this way the unfortunate native helps to bring about his own extinction. This fear of magic has always been strong in the minds of primitive people.

Games of all kinds are played by the children, who practise throwing spears, and also an amusing little implement called the "weet-weet", because it has the form of a kangaroo rat. Then a day comes when the boys are grown up, and are initiated and become men. Dances are performed by the men before the novitiates to typify essential qualities. The dog and kangaroo are shown for endurance and speed. The boy has one of his front teeth knocked out to teach him to bear pain. The bull roarer, a long flat leaf-shaped piece of wood scored across, is whirled round on a thong, and the whistling noise it makes is thought to be the voice of a god. It is the boy's introduction to the spiritual life of the tribe; to a knowledge of the Mysteries, and of the High God who lives in the Sky.

When an Australian is born it is assumed that he brings with him a *churinga*; these are long flat pieces of wood or stone with rounded ends, marked with various totem devices, and considered sacred objects. These are deposited in caves, and only brought out for ceremonies.

THE FIRST CAVE-DWELLERS

The Australians have various methods of disposing of their dead, but burial is the most general. With the bodies are interred weapons, food, and a drinking-cup for use in the happy hunting-grounds, so that in one more detail they resemble the Moustier man of La Chapelle-aux-Saints, with whose remains a flint hand-axe was found.

We need not continue these comparisons, but we hope that those we have given may help to build up a picture of what the surroundings of Moustier man may have been like.

At the end of the second chapter we gave a sketch of Hand-axe man, and tried to show that his most urgent need was food; that unless he hunted, he starved, and could not depend, as we do, on a shop round the corner, and the effort of other men. This was the material side of his life; but what of the spiritual? We shall be quite wrong if we think of primitive man as being only concerned with food, because man has always demanded some other interest.

We have the very early belief in a life hereafter, in the happy hunting-grounds, where conditions were kindlier, and there was more opportunity to expand. The Chapelle-aux-Saints burial, with flint implements to hand, for use in the spirit world, points to this. How did this come about? Primitive man, or woman, curled round asleep by his fire, dreamed dreams and saw visions; his spirit seemed to separate from his body, and he joined old friends who were dead, and with them followed in the chase, or did the wonderful things we all do in our dreams. When he awakened and rubbed sleepy eyes to find his own fireside, he told his friends of his adventures; that so and so was not dead but a spirit in a wonderful world. We can see the beginnings of ancestor worship. An acute fit of indigestion, coming after too much mammoth, would have provided the nightmare, and its equivalent horrors, and an underworld of bad spirits.

The man of imagination would have polished up the tale, and filled in the gaps, and gaining much renown thereby, became the medicine man or priest. He would exorcise the evil spirits, for a consideration, or bring messages from the good ones. At other times, in the excitement of hunting, the voice of the man would be echoed back from the hills, where by search he could find no other people. It was magical and mysterious, just as it

THE BEGINNING OF MAGIC

was when his own face looked back at him from the pool to which he stooped to drink.

The sun, moon, and stars gave him cause for wonder, and glaciers mightier than the Baltoro seemed to him alive, as they crept to the sea. He made them gods. Perhaps on a stormy day he looked through a rift in the clouds, and saw others heaped and peaked into glittering pinnacles lighted by a sun he could not see himself, and thought of it all as the pleasant country of the land of dreams. The long nights and storms made him fearful.

Chapter IV

ARTISTS OF THE OLD STONE AGE

AURIGNAC MAN

WITH Moustier man the Older (Lower and Middle) Palaeolithic Period came to an end, and the next phase we shall consider will be the Upper Palaeolithic.

Two things mark the change from the earlier periods: the use of a multitude of new types of tools, all made on small blades of flint, and the arrival of Modern man (*Homo sapiens*). Blade tools are the first industrial revolution. As we have seen, some of the earliest of men's tools, the Hand-axes, were beautifully made, but you could only make one of them from a single block of flint. Mousterian tools were the same. Each time Mousterian man made a spear-head he had to knock off a large flake from a specially shaped lump of flint. If he wanted another spear-head he had to prepare another lump of flint to get the flake which he wanted. The Great Upper Palaeolithic discovery was that from one block of flint you could get a great many single parallel-sided flakes. These are called blades by the archaeologist because they look like the blade of a knife. Figs. *34, 35* show the blocks of flint from which these blades were removed, called blade cores, and some blades which have been knocked off them. From each of these blades a separate flint tool could be made and a great variety of these tools are found in the Upper Palaeolithic.

In fact we recognize the difference between the various people who lived in the Upper Palaeolithic by the different shapes of tool they made from these small blades. Behind the discovery of the blade tool lies another discovery. We have seen that Acheulean man found he could make thinner hand-axes by hitting a piece of flint with a wooden rod instead of battering it with another block of stone. In just the same way Upper Palaeolithic man discovered that if you took a strong pointed bone or stone rod and pressed hard enough on the flint block a narrow parallel-sided blade would jump off. This is called pressure flaking. Upper Palaeolithic man carefully shaped a block of flint

BLADE TOOLS

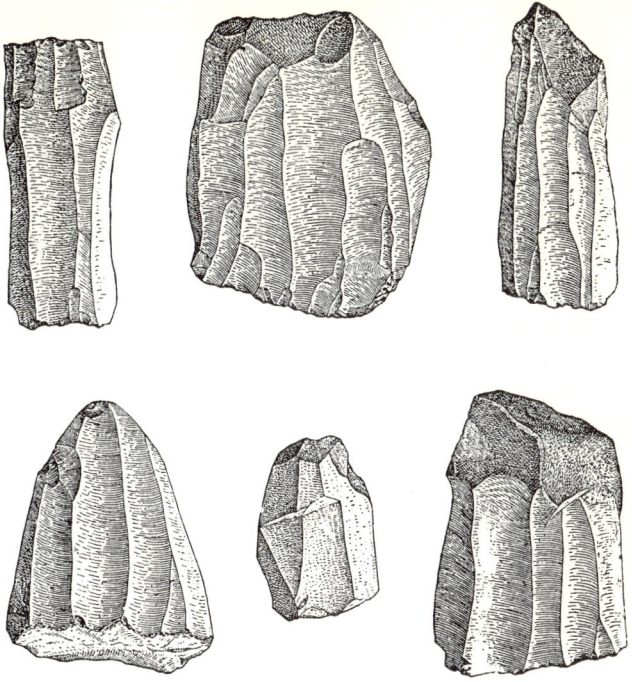

34 Blade cores

to form a cylinder or a pyramid, that is to say with one flat end or two flat ends, as can be seen in our illustration. By pressure flaking on the very edge of the flat end he was able to remake blades all round so that the blade core got smaller and smaller. Different sizes of blades came off the core as it got smaller, but all these could be used to make tools.

We have already said that the other important Upper Palaeolithic event was the arrival of Modern man (*Homo sapiens*). Indeed even with the first Upper Palaeolithic people known in Europe, named after Aurignac, a cave in the south of France, we already find two or three different races of prehistoric man, differing from each other as Englishmen do from Frenchmen. Now, blade tools seem to have been Modern man's first discovery, and all the Upper Palaeolithic blade tools were made by Modern man. However, the earliest blade tools we know come from a cave at Mount Carmel in Palestine, where they

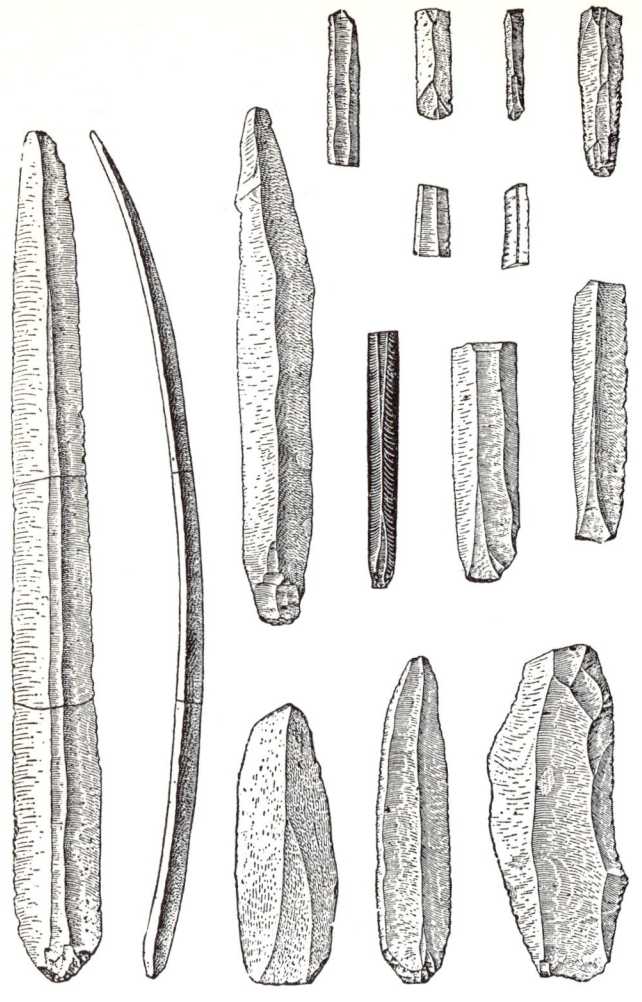

35 Flint blades

are found mixed up with the tools of Mousterian man. In another cave at Mount Carmel, where all the tools of Mousterian man were found, the archaeologists discovered some buried human skeletons, called *Paleoanthropus Palestinus*, which seemed to belong to a mixed race of people. In some ways they looked like Mousterian man, in some ways like *Homo sapiens*.

THE ARRIVAL OF *HOMO SAPIENS*

So that it seems that blade tools were invented in Palestine by a special type of man who was less like Mousterian or Neanderthal man than the sort of a man we know today all over the world. Archaeologists are not sure that this is quite true, but, shortly after this important event, Modern man, carrying his blade tools with him, spread suddenly right across Europe and Africa and India and all the Mousterian men disappear. So Mount Carmel provides us with an important clue to the History of Man.

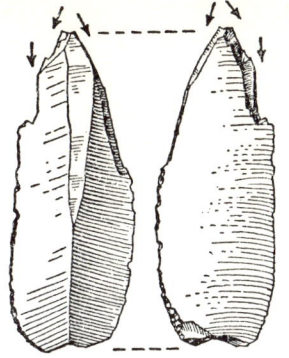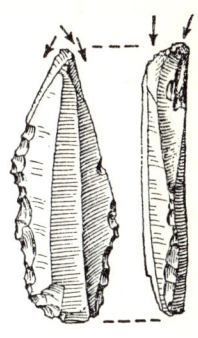

36 Two flint burins, chisels or gravers

Let us now see how the earliest Modern man in Europe lived. In France and England there are three main peoples whom we know as Aurignac, Solutré, and Madeleine man. They seem to have occupied the same caves one after another so that we find their relics in different layers in these caves, always in the same order; the Aurignac men are always the ones in the lowest layers and therefore the earliest occupants of the caves.

The Aurignac men were cave-dwellers but lived as well in the

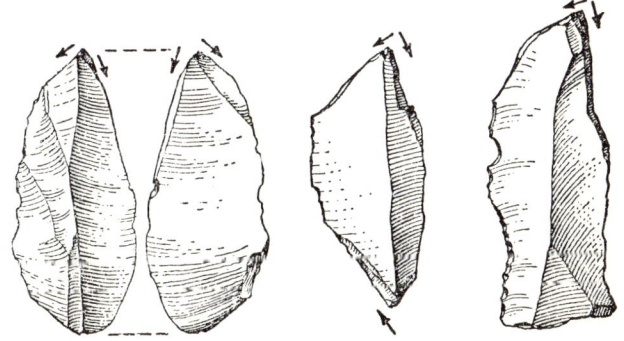

37 Two flint burins, chisels or gravers

38 Type of huts suggested by Aurignac drawings

AURIGNAC TOOLS

open; their camps have been found in the newer Loess (p. 33), and for this reason they have been called the Loess men. If, as has been thought, the Bushmen may be the descendants of the Aurignac men, we may perhaps assume that the Loess men had the same sort of huts. These the Bushmen constructed, much as the gipsy does today, with a framework of bent sticks covered with skins (*38*). Darwin wrote of the "toldos" of the Indians near Bahia Blanca, South America: "These are round like ovens, and covered with hides; by the mouth of each a tapering chuzo (spear) was struck in the ground."

39 The spokeshave

The Aurignac people improved on the Moustier flint implements; we find several sorts of scrapers, knives, and gravers; the latter a tool for engraving, which must be the first tool made by man for a special purpose. These gravers or burins are very easy to recognize because of their chisel ends, shown by the arrows in our illustration. There are also scrapers, flaked ingeniously into very useful spokeshaves, and fig. *39* shows a man shaving down the shaft for a lance. The Aurignac man, judged by the variety of tools which he possessed, must have been a clever workman making all sorts of things; remember all his woodwork has disappeared, and we only find now the imperishable flint, and some bone implements. With his burin, or graving tool, he easily cut pieces out of reindeer horns, and made arrow- and spear-heads. This use of bone marks another step forward, and from now on we shall find many examples of this new material. Bone bodkins were used to pierce skins and pass sinews through, then the bodkin had a blunt barb formed at one end to pull the thong through like a crochet-needle, and

ARTISTS OF THE OLD STONE AGE

so led up to the bone needles of Upper Solutré times (*48*). Later on we shall find barbed harpoons. The Aurignac man used the bow and arrow—we know this because shaft-straighteners have been found, bored to take shafts of different thicknesses. These were used as shown in fig. *40*. The shaft, after having been shaved clean, would have been passed over a wood fire to make it supple, and then slipped through the hole of the shaft-straightener, which is cut obliquely. It can be seen that pressure applied on the handle would bend the shaft in any desired direction. The natives of the Punjab in India still straighten bamboos in this way, only their shaft-straightener is a substantial post set strongly in the ground. Through this there are bored holes, and the warmed bamboo is put through these, and curves removed by bending the stem in an opposite direction. The Eskimo, on the other hand, follows the Aurignac way. The early bow, like the early gun, was probably not very effective, and the spear must have remained the great weapon. Darwin, writing of the Indians from the south of Chile, said: "The only weapon of an Indian is a very long bamboo or chuzo, ornamented with ostrich feathers, and pointed by a sharp spearhead." The boring of holes in the shaft-straightener, and the use of the bow, suggests that the Aurignac men used the bow-drill both to bore holes and make fire, as the Eskimos do (*41*).

The Aurignac men hunted for their food, as those of Le Moustier had done and people had not yet learned how to domesticate animals, or grow foodstuffs. The reindeer were very

40   Shaft straightening

AURIGNAC HUNTING

plentiful; so much is this the case that the French archaeologists talk of the Upper Palaeolithic as the Age of the Reindeer. The climate was improving, and as the Fourth Glacial Period receded, game became more plentiful. The horse was eaten in those days, and in France huge mounds of the bones have been discovered, left as the débris of many Aurignac feasts. Even as late as 1831 Darwin wrote of South American troops: "Mare's flesh is the only food which the soldiers have when on an expedition."

41 The bow-drill

Here is an account of how the horses may have been caught, taken from Falconer's *Patagonia*: "The Indians drive troops of wild horses into a 'Corral' encompassed by high cliffs between 30 and 40 feet high, excepting at one spot where the entrance lies. This is guarded to keep them secure."

At Ivinghoe Beacon there is a curious cleft in the hills, which tradition says was a wolf trap in olden days, and its form certainly lends to it the appearance of a corral.

There is another fact which goes to show that the conditions of life were becoming easier. Man and perhaps woman began to draw, and to do so extremely well. It is a most interesting fact, and one which should be noted, that the tribe was content to let these people spend their time in this way. One can imagine that the Moustier or Neanderthal man, very much occupied with the struggle for existence at the end of the Fourth Glacial Period, would have dealt sternly with the budding artist, who desired to cut his share of the "chores", because he wanted to draw; but in Aurignac times he was allowed to do so, and drawing and sculpture extended into the Madeleine Period. These drawings and paintings are something altogether beyond the art of ordinary savage people. The Australians, for instance, decorate their wooden shields with red, white, and black, wavy lines, and lozenges, which have a pleasantly decorative effect; but of the polychrome figures which marked the culmination of Madeleine art, the Abbé Breuil has written: "et qui place les vieux peintres des âges glyptiques bien au-dessus des animaliers de toutes les civilisations de l'orient classique et de la Grèce". So here is another problem; it is quite certain that endless experiment must have been made before the artists could have arrived at such marvellous dexterity. How did these wonderful people jump out of the void of time? These drawings were first discovered by a Spanish nobleman, Marcellino de Santuola, who lived at Santander, Spain. He was interested in archaeology, and was digging one day in the cave of Altamira, near his home. With him was his little daughter, who, tired of watching the digging, wandered round the cave, and alarmed her father by calling out "Toros! Toros!" Bulls in a cave would be somewhat alarming, and S. Santuola, hurrying to the rescue, found the small girl gazing at the roof of the cavern. Here he discovered drawings and paintings of bulls, bison, deer, horses, and many other animals, some life-size. The discovery threw the archaeological world into commotion—most discoveries do; people could not believe that these really wonderful drawings could have been produced as such an early stage in the world's history. Just as the Neanderthal man was not at first believed to be a man, and some early flint tools are not yet generally recognized as the work of man, so the Altamira drawings were received with scepticism. That stage has been passed through now, many books have been written, innumerable papers read before learned societies, and other drawings discovered in certain French caves, which have convinced the archaeologists that in the Altamira cave are authentic works of the earliest period of the world's art; and we owe the discovery to one small girl who called "Toros!" in alarm to her father.

The old painters seem to have started with drawings in outline like fig. *42*, and then later in Madeleine times they passed on to solid colour(*1*), and some of these have an engraved outline. If our readers are interested they should try to see a book by the Abbé Breuil, a distinguished Frenchman, who has made a special study of this work.

We must pass on to a consideration of what purpose the drawings served. At Altamira they are in a dark cave, which

AURIGNAC PAINTINGS AND CARVINGS

has a total length of 280 metres (a metre is about 3 feet 3⅜ inches). There is no light in the cave, and the figures occur over all the walls. They cannot be seen now without a light, and a lamp must have been used when they were painted; so we have another discovery, that man had artificial illumination in Upper Paleolithic times. A dark cave, though, does not make a good picture gallery for display, and it does not seem as if the Cave were the National Gallery of the day.

42   Aurignac drawing

It is thought that carving in the round came first, then low relief, then outline drawing (engraving), though all these styles were no doubt contemporary for some time. Statuettes are common in Aurignac, and rare in Solutré times, and engravings reached perfection in the Madeleine period.

Many suggestions have been made as to the uses of the paintings; one is that as most of the animals drawn are those which were hunted for food, the paintings formed a magic which placed the animals under the power of the medicine man of the tribe. Many of the animals are drawn with arrows sticking in their bodies; on some the heart is shown in red. This was a practice which lingered on till recent times—to make a model of your enemy and stick it full of pins; that is, if you were a spiteful person and wished him harm.

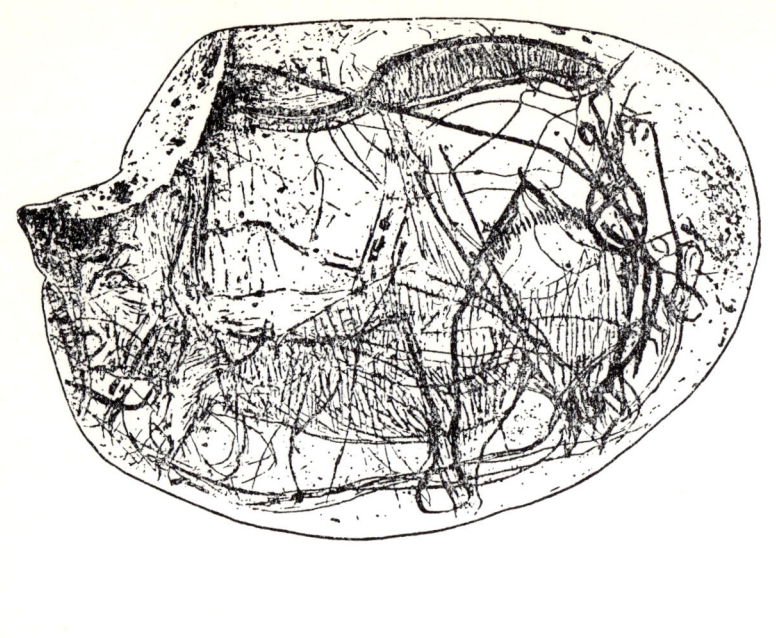

43–46 An Aurignacian artist's sketch-book on a stone (43

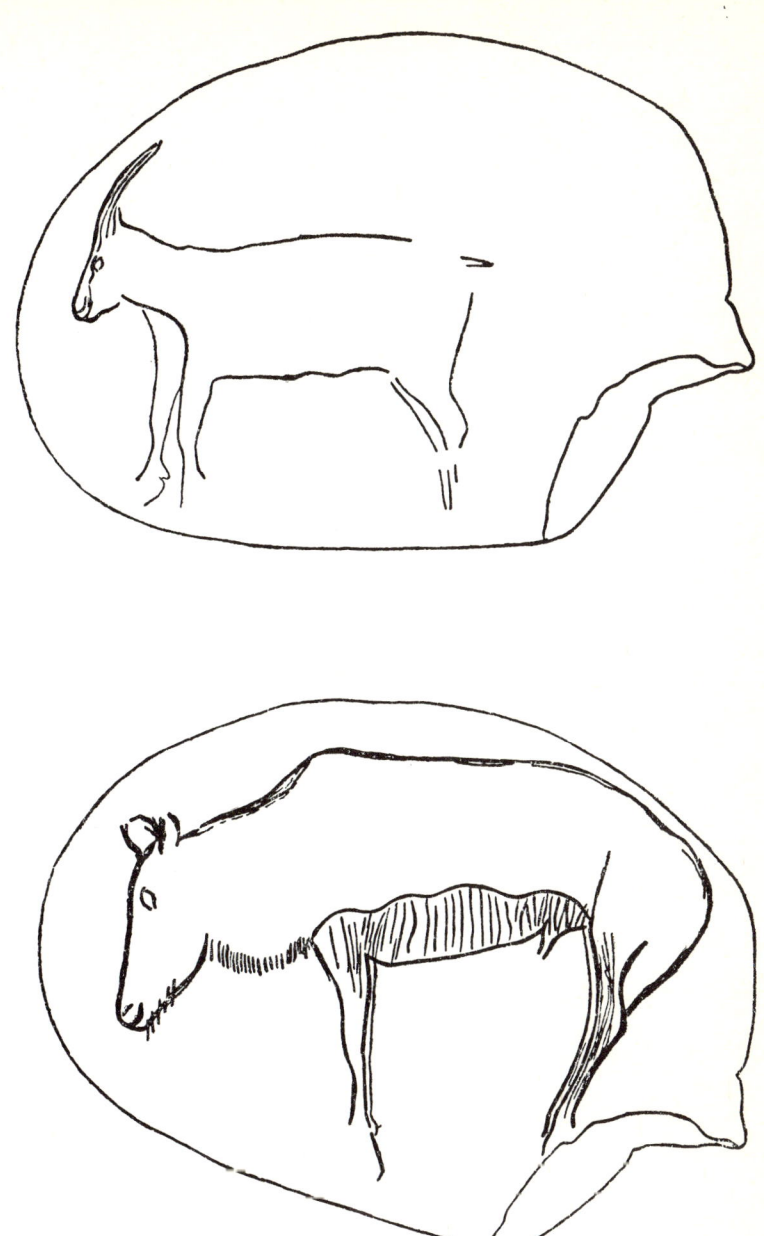

with three of the sketches drawn out separately. *After Movius*

ARTISTS OF THE OLD STONE AGE

These Aurignac drawings may therefore have been used to help the hunters. The head-man of the tribe, or perhaps the medicine man, drew an animal, and then you drew in the arrows which killed the animal. Afterwards you went out and killed a real animal brought to you by the magic of the artist. This is called Sympathetic Magic. We are also able to find the sketch-books of the artists who drew these animals on the cave walls. They are pebbles with a smooth surface where they practised their drawings. An Aurignac sketch-book only had two pages—the two sides of the pebble—so that lots of different drawings are put on top of one another on the same page. Fig. 43 shows one page of the sketch-book, with all the different drawings that have been found on it copied out separately in the other pictures. If you look carefully at the sketch-book you can see all these drawings.

The Aurignac men were accomplished sculptors and modelled quite good little figures in the round, about 4 to 5 inches high, and as well in low relief. A curious detail is that the faces are not rendered; in their drawings and paintings, they seldom if ever presented the human figure, except occasionally by grotesque faces. This may have arisen from the fact that primitive people think that a picture or figure of a man becomes part of his personality. If damage be done to it, then it reacts on the man, so any recognizable portrait of an individual doubles his risks. In the case of the animals drawn this was desirable to the Aurignac man.

Another suggestion is that the mammoth, the bison, or any of the animals drawn, might have been the Totem of the tribe; that they were grouped in clans, as the brothers of the bison perhaps. This, as we have seen, was a practice with the Australians, the Red Indians of America, and the boy scouts of today. The Altamira cave in this case would have been the temple in which were preserved totem symbols. One peculiarity at Altamira is that one drawing is frequently found made on the top of another. The interiors of the loftier caves must have first turned men's ideas in the direction of fine building; something which should be nobler than their little huts, and suitable for ceremonies. In the painted caves of France and Spain are found the imprints of hands. A hand has evidently been smeared with colour, and then printed on to the surface of the rock or the

PAINTING AND MAGIC

hand placed there first, and then colour dusted over it, leaving a white silhouette when the hand was removed. Many of the hands show traces of mutilation; that is, the end of a finger has been cut off at the joint. This dismal practice was widely spread and lasted until recent times. It was a form of sacrifice. It existed among the Australians, the Bushmen of South Africa, and some of the Red Indians, for example, and was practised for a variety of causes, generally as a sign of grief, and to implore the better favour of the gods in future. It seems reasonable, then, to suppose that the Aurignac people lost the fingers, which must have been so useful to them, in some such way.

The Aurignac women, and perhaps the men as well, appear to have been fond of trying to make themselves beautiful. Here in Great Britain, at Paviland Cave in Wales, were found perforated wolves' teeth for use as a necklace, and an ivory bracelet made by sawing rings through the hollow base of a mammoth's tusk. We can also be quite sure that so gifted a people must have experimented in the production of music. We know that they had bows and arrows. The twang of the bow led to our piano. The latter is only a harp on its side, the strings of which are struck with hammers instead of being plucked with the fingers, and the harp is the bow with many strings; the reed and pipe would lead to the horn, and the drum has always been the great instrument of the native musician. At Alpera, in Spain, are some wonderful paintings of Upper Palaeolithic date, and here are shown figures of women who seem to be dancing. Now dancing means some sort of music, and the cheerful tum-tum of a drum is almost necessary if one is to keep time. In the original Alpera drawings are figures which appear to be wearing quaint head-dresses; perhaps this was a masquerade. If all this sounds improbable, remember their wonderful drawings; to such people much is possible. Dancing has always been an accomplishment of savage people. Darwin wrote of a "corrobery", or dancing party, of the aborigines in Australia, held at night by the light of fires, the women and children squatting round as spectators. An "Emu dance, in which each man extended his arm in a bent manner, like the neck of that bird. In another dance, one man imitated the movements of a kangaroo grazing in the woods, whilst a second crawled up, and pretended to spear him." In this way they dramatized their everyday life.

ARTISTS OF THE OLD STONE AGE

SOLUTRÉ MAN

The next division of the Upper Palaeolithic is the one which the archaeologists have named after Solutré, near Mâcon (Saône-et-Loire) in France. Solutré man appears to have lived in England, because evidences of his industry have been found at Paviland Cave in South Wales, and Creswell Crags, Derbyshire; as well as in France, Central Europe, and the North of Spain, but not in Italy. The Solutré men may have been horse hunters who invaded Europe along the open grasslands of the Loess (p. 32). It has been assumed that they were a warlike race, because of the very beautiful flint lance-heads which have been found; some of these are like an assegai, and would have been deadly weapons (47). They are beautifully flaked flints, shaped like a laurel leaf, from which they get their name (*pointe en feuille de laurier*); the smaller types like a willow leaf, and so called (*pointe en feuille de saule*). B shows the highest Palaeolithic development of flint flaking, the *pointe à cran*, or shouldered point, by which a primitive barb was formed. C is an arrow-head with a flint tang which could be bound on to the shaft.

Flint flaking came to its highest point of development in the Old Stone Age in Solutré times, though it was to revive again later in the New Stone, or Neolithic Age. The Solutré people made borers, scrapers, and arrow-heads; they, in fact, carried on the Aurignac traditions; bone and ivory were used; and painting and drawing continued. Perhaps the most wonderful development of this

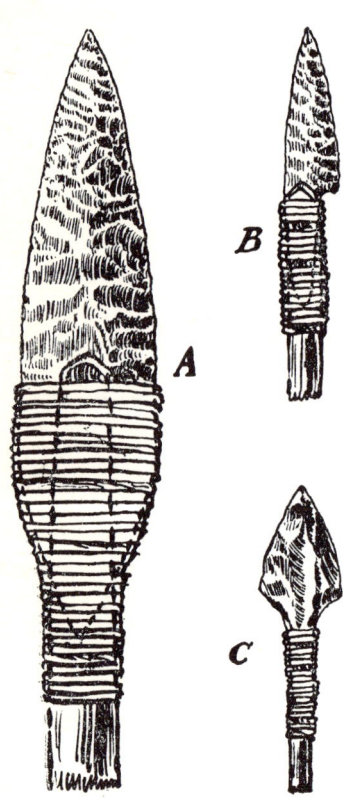

47 Solutré flints

SOLUTREAN ARROWS AND NEEDLES

time was the bone needle; at the beginning the sewing had been done in the same way that a shoemaker sews the sole of a shoe now, by boring a hole with a bone awl, and then passing a thread through. Of course, the Aurignac men had not any thread, but must have used fine sinews in this way. The next step was to hook the end of the awl so that the sinew could be pulled

48 Making of bone needles

through, using the awl first to pierce the hole, and then as a crochet-needle to pull the thread through. The final step was to combine the two operations into one by the use of the needle, which pierced the hole, and carried the thread through itself (*48* A, B, and C). To realize the joy of a Solutré woman who first used a needle, let us imagine ourselves sewing today like a shoemaker, punching holes one at a time.

Fig. *48* shows a Solutré needlemaker at work; first she cut a splinter of bone out of reindeer horn, as at 1. This was done by cutting a groove on each side with a flint graving tool, as at 2. The splinter was then shaved down with a scraper, as 3, and polished with a piece of stone, as at 4, and the eye bored with a flint borer, as 5. You can see, at the British Museum, the actual needles and the implements with which they were made. A sewing machine is a mechanically operated needle. At the British Museum you can see the start of the whole long business which led up to the sewing machine. Madeleine women later on used hollow bones as needle-cases.

Though the Fourth Glacial Period was now long past and the weather was gradually becoming more temperate, it did not

ARTISTS OF THE OLD STONE AGE

improve in a regular way. The weather was colder than in Aurignac times, and the mammoth and reindeer were still found in Europe.

MADELEINE MAN

We can now pass on to the Madeleine or Magdalenian men, who succeeded those of Solutré. The typical station of the industry is on the Vézère, not far from the Castle of La Madeleine, hence the name. The Solutré man excelled in flint flaking, and the majority of the implements he made were in this material. The Madeleine man used flint for his scrapers, borers, and gravers, and finished them roughly. For other implements he made, he preferred bone and ivory. This detail at first may not seem of much importance, in reality it is as vital as if today we gave up steel and concrete and started using some new material. Flint was to have a wonderful renaissance later on in Neolithic

49   Magdalenian portrait of a woman

times before it slowly gave way to bronze. In many ways the Madeleine men appear to have been the descendants of those of Aurignac.

We have said that all the Upper Palaeolithic Peoples belong to what we call Modern man. With the Early Aurignac and Solutré men it is difficult to get any idea what they looked like. The Madeleine man does occasionally draw pictures of himself, and we show one drawing that a man did of his wife all those years ago (*49*). She is sitting down in the cave and she seems to be wearing a cape round her head, some sort of boots on her feet, and clothing rather like a boiler suit covering her from head to foot. Her nose is slightly turned up. This retroussé nose, as it is called, seems to have been a feature of some Madeleine men and women, for the newly discovered painting of a man at Angles-sur-l'Anglin has just the same feature.

Madeleine man appears to have been widely distributed over Europe. At Altamira, in Spain, he added the masterpieces of painting to the earlier drawings of the Aurignac men. He lived in France, Germany, and Belgium, and here in England his handiwork has been found at Kent's Cavern in Devon, and Creswell Crags in Derbyshire. We are so anchored nowadays, with our houses to live in, and farms to raise food-stuffs, that it is difficult to realize this widespread distribution of prehistoric man, but in reality he needed far larger areas of land on which to hunt and find food.

Madeleine man made his spear- and arrow-heads in ivory and reindeer horn; these were spliced on to wooden shafts and consisted of long lance-like points (*50*, 1). From these developed harpoons, first with one row of barbs, and then with two, as 2 and 3. This was a most useful discovery, that the barb would hold a fish after it had been speared; one can imagine the disgust of the early fisherman who lost his catch off the plain lance; his joy when he held it on the barbed harpoon. The first good fisherman's tale must have started with some such exploit. Spearing fish sounds a little unreal today, but there is an interesting account in Sir Walter Scott's *Redgauntlet*, of sport carried on in this way on horseback. "They chased the fish at full gallop, and struck them with their barbed spears." The scene is laid in the estuary of the Solway at low water, when the "waters had receded from the large and level space of sand, through

ARTISTS OF THE OLD STONE AGE

which a stream, now feeble and fordable, found its way to the ocean". Madeleine man must have had many a good day's sport like this. Out of the barb of the harpoon, the fish-hook must have developed. All this was possible in bone, though a rarity in flint. Bone lends itself to decoration, and so the Madeleine man incised simple designs on his lance-heads. Smaller bone points have been found which suggest arrow-heads, but no bows. These being wooden would have decayed. This influence of material on design is very important; it is a very false and bad art which wastes material or tortures it into a shape which is unsuitable, so these early Madeleine men were proper designers, in that they used their material in a right way. The harpoons show them to have been fishermen, and there are Madeleine drawings of seal and salmon engraved on stone and also on bone implements. We illustrate two of these drawings.

The first (*51*) shows a man diving into a river, or the sea, which is full of fish. This is very poorly drawn. The second (*52*) is a beautiful drawing of some seals and some snake-like fish. On the end of the two bones in this illustration you can see where

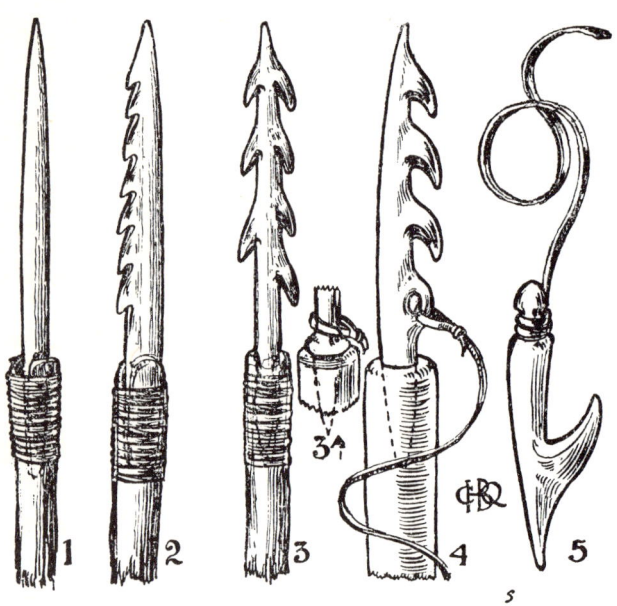

50   Spears and harpoons

HARPOONING FISH

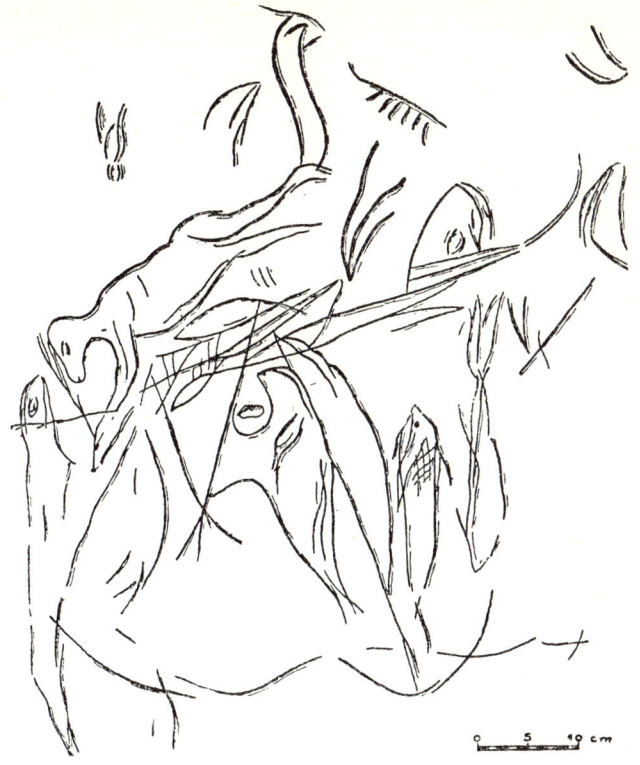

51 A man diving into a river. Engraved on a Magdalenian bone tool

the artist has drawn the harpoons with which he hopes to kill the seals. One expects that the rivers then would have been like those in Western Canada today, where the salmon come up from the sea in tremendous quantities.

Nos. 3 A and 4 (*50*) show another interesting development of the harpoon. Madeleine specimens have been found with a movable head, and this suggests that they were used in the same way as the harpoons of the Eskimo. No. 5 is our suggestion of how the fish-hook developed out of the barb of the harpoon. As there are many other points of resemblance between the Eskimo and the Madeleine man, we will see if any useful comparisons can be drawn.

The Eskimos are very widely distributed, as they must be, because they live by hunting. They depend on the seal, whale,

ARTISTS OF THE OLD STONE AGE

and walrus for food and clothing, and these they hunt all along the Arctic coasts from Greenland to Alaska. They are a very gifted, pleasant people, who have not any idea of war, because their main concern is a struggle for existence amidst ice and snow. They do not work iron, though in latter days they have made use of any pieces which they could get hold of from traders. The Eskimo works in bone and wood in a really wonderful way, as we shall see. He also appears to have inherited the skill of the Madeleine people in drawing. Dr. Nansen writes of an Eskimo from Cape York, who "took a pencil, a thing he had never seen before, and sketched the coast-line along Smith's Sound from his birthplace northwards with astonishing accuracy".

We will start with their methods of hunting. Seals are speared at blow-holes in the ice, but far more interesting are the methods by which they are harpooned in the open summer seas. The Eskimo uses his kayak (*53*); this is a boat which varies somewhat in the various districts, but in all is constructed on the same principle. On the west coast of Greenland it is about 17 feet long, and made of driftwood on a frame (*54*), which is all bound together with thongs, and covered with sealskin. The kayak is decked over, and paddled with a double-bladed paddle. If we assume that the early Madeleine men were as clever as the Eskimos, and first made an open canoe (*32*), they would have found, as they left the rivers and ventured to sea, that the deck

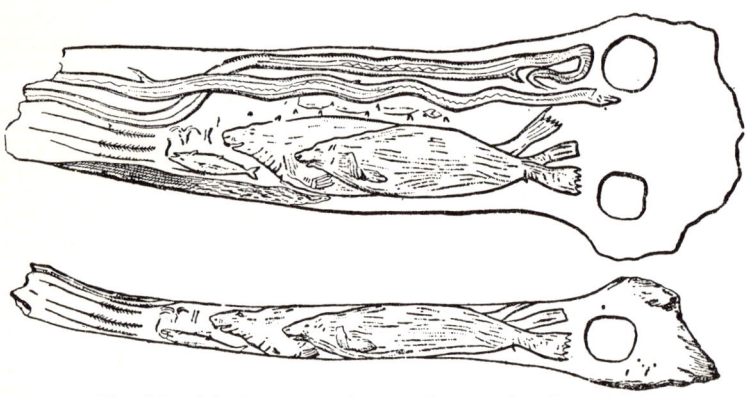

52 Magdalenian engravings on bones of seals and fish

ESKIMO SEAL HUNTING

53   The kayak

was an improvement. The harpoon with movable head (50, 4) suggests that they did go to sea, and attacked some larger quarry than the salmon. If they harpooned the seal with No. 3, the first convulsive plunge would have snapped off the head, and this was a precious possession. The head was made then to fit into a bone holder on the end of the lance, so that when the seal dived he wrenched it out of the holder only to find that it was still attached to the shaft by a leather thong. The Eskimo uses two harpoons, which are very beautiful developments of this idea.

Fig. 55, 1, shows their bladder dart. The head is removable and attached by a thong to the centre of the shaft, where in addition they fix a blown-up bladder. When the seal dives he is encumbered by the shaft, which is at right angles to the thong, and the bladder, which also marks his position when he comes to the surface.

No. 2 shows the Eskimo harpoon. This had in old days an ivory head, tipped with flint, fitted on to a bone shaft. This latter is protected from snapping, by being attached to the wooden shaft with thongs in a sort of ball and socket joint. The line is attached to the ivory head, and then passes over a stud on the harpoon shaft; the loose line is carried on a holder on the kayak in front of the Eskimo, and the end is attached to a large sealskin

ARTISTS OF THE OLD STONE AGE

54 Framework of kayak

float which rests at his back. The harpoon is propelled with a thrower in the same way that the Australian hurls his spears (*27, 28*). The head of the harpoon buries itself in the seal, and is so attached to the line that it turns at right angles in the wound. It is at once wrenched off the bone shaft, and the position of the seal is noted by the float, which is thrown overboard. The wooden shaft floats and is picked up.

As there are many very beautiful ivory or bone harpoon-throwers of Madeleine times, it seems fair to assume that the seal was hunted then as it is by the Eskimo today.

Fig. 55, 3, shows the bird dart which is used with a thrower. The forward projecting barbs kill the bird if the actual point misses. All these weapons are carried by the Eskimo on the deck of the kayak, neatly fitted under thongs and ivory studs.

The Eskimo's clothing is of sealskin, and his coat is arranged to fit closely around the circular rim of the hole in the deck in which he sits. He can be tumbled right over by a rough sea, and yet right himself with a turn of the paddle.

The Madeleine man had bone needles, and his clothing may have been like this.

At the British Museum there is a sledge made of driftwood, with bone platings on the runners, all tied up with thongs. It should be seen to realize how primitive man managed without nails and screws. There are also kayaks and a model of the umiak or women's boat. Fig. 56 shows

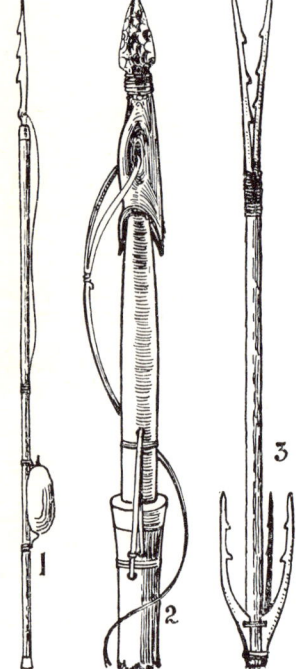

55 Eskimo bladder dart, harpoon, and bird dart

DRAWING OF HUTS AND TENTS

56   Eskimo game

an Eskimo game played rather like cup and ball. A very much simplified Polar bear is carved in ivory and pierced with many holes; the bear has to be caught through one of the holes on the end of the stick.

The boring of holes brings up the question of whether Madeleine man used the bow-drill. Small ivory rods have been found, perforated at one end, with a slit at the other shaped into a mouth. This is thought to have been the bow. The bowstring was tied through the hole at one end, given a twist round the drill, and the bow then being bent, a loop in the bowstring was slipped into the notched end of the bow, and kept the latter bent. Fig. *41* shows how the drill could then be rotated. Such drills are used by the Eskimo, and many other primitive people today, both to bore holes and produce fire by friction.

Drawings have been discovered which are thought to represent tents or huts, and suggest that in Madeleine times improvements had been made on those of the Aurignac men, as shown in fig. *38*. This round beehive form, made perhaps of willow withies, would have been weak in the crown, if the tent was of any size, yet it could be constructed very simply anywhere that saplings were found. One of the Madeleine drawings suggests a type (*57*). Almost all the early hut builders seem to have dug a hole of circular shape in the ground. The earth removed was heaped up round the outside. In the centre of the hole a roof-tree was set up, formed of the trunk of a tree, with a fork perhaps left at the top. Around this saplings were placed, their feet stuck into the

ARTISTS OF THE OLD STONE AGE

surrounding mound, with the tops leaning against the roof-tree. These formed the rafters, and if in between these were interlaced smaller boughs, it is quite easy to see that the whole could be covered with skins, or rough grass thatch. Quite a comfortable little house could be made in this way, and we know that it is a type which was general in Neolithic times.

Other Madeleine drawings suggest a tepe(*58*), and this is a form of hut which is constructed by the North American Indians.

The Madeleine people had their winter quarters in caves and rock shelters, and the period is named after the rock-shelters of La Madeleine on the banks of the Vézère. Did Madeleine man, as he slowly travelled to the north, take with him a memory of the rock-shelters of France, and hand down a building tradition to the Eskimo of today? They have very interesting rock houses, and others which are constructed in a skilful way with blocks of snow. Stone lamps have been discovered, which suggest that the Madeleine man not only lighted but warmed his houses, as the Eskimo does today, by burning fat in a stone lamp with a moss wick.

57 Type of huts suggested by Madeleine drawings

ESKIMO HOUSES

58   Type of hut suggested by Madeleine drawings

Fig. 59 shows the skin tent which the Eskimo uses on his summer wanderings. The plan resembles that of the houses; there is the semicircular bed-place at A, and a central gangway at B, with cooking pots at the sides at C. The diagram shows how the tent is made with poles and covered with skins, the front portion being of membrane to admit light. Large stones serve to hold down the skins. We have included these drawings because we want to get as many representative

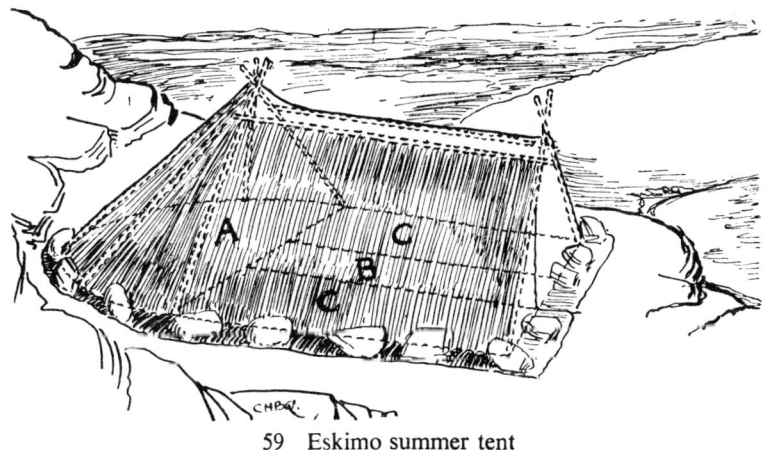

59   Eskimo summer tent

ARTISTS OF THE OLD STONE AGE

60 Digging-stick

types as we can of primitive dwelling-places. We shall find it useful later on.

The Madeleine man, like the Eskimo, may have used his lamp for cooking, but here is an interesting description by Darwin of some Tahitians who prepared a meal in another way: "Having made a small fire of sticks, they placed a score of stones, of about the size of cricket balls, on the burning wood. In about ten minutes the sticks were consumed, and the stones hot. They had previously folded up in small parcels of leaves, pieces of beef, fish, ripe and unripe bananas, and the tops of the wild arum. These green parcels were laid in a layer between two layers of the hot stones, and the whole then covered up with earth, so that no smoke or steam could escape. In about a quarter of an hour, the whole was most deliciously cooked." This was a method used later on in Neolithic times. The Madeleine man may have used the reindeer for food in the winter, by drying the flesh over a wood fire,

61   A wall painting of a bison. *After Breuil*

ANIMAL ART

62 The head of a galloping horse

and then pounding it up, and preserving it by pouring over hot fat, rather like the pemmican of the Indian and Eskimo.

We cannot be sure whether the Madeleine people had started cultivating the soil. Perforated stones have been found which may have been used to load the digging-stick (60). This is the method the Bushmen adopt, and Darwin mentioned the use of the digging-stick in Chile, to dig up roots, though this does not mean cultivating them.

The Madeleine Period marked the highest development of the art of prehistoric man. The paintings are of astonishing merit; without being great sticklers for detail, these old painters caught the very spirit of the animals they painted. The mammoth swings along alive from the tip of his trunk to the end of his tufted tail. The bison and boar charge; the reindeer and red deer move in a slow, easy canter. The drawings are proof of the immensely developed power of detailed observation which came to the hunter as part of his craft, and which is different from the sympathy shown in later days, when animals were domesticated. Fig. *1* shows a bison from the Altamira Cave in Spain, and fig. *61* another bison, this time drawn in black and white, from a French cave. In the last drawing you can clearly see the arrows drawn in to kill the beast.

The artists of those days used reds and browns, blacks and yellows, and were adepts at producing high-lights, half-tones, and shadow. They appear to have started with a black outline.

ARTISTS OF THE OLD STONE AGE

and then to have filled in the body of the work, adding tone, or wiping away colour to get the effect of lights. The figures are often of life size, and their vigour makes us wish that we could draw animals in such a living way.

M. Daleau has found, in France, red oxide of iron, which formed the basis of one of the colours, the pestles with which it was ground, and the shoulder-blades of animals that served as palettes. Brushes were used, and would not have been difficult to make. The paints were carried in little tubes made of reindeer horn; truly there is nothing new under the sun, and we shall find some day, perhaps, a catalogue of a Madeleine artists' colour-man. The Madeleine engravings on ivory, sometimes on the handles of their shaft-straighteners, were just as wonderful as the paintings. We have said that these artists caught the very spirit of the animals they drew, and to do this they realized that it was necessary to compose, or design, their shapes and out-lines. Today we can photograph a horse while galloping, and the resulting print will not convey the sense of action that the Palaeolithic artist has obtained in fig. *62*. This is because the human eye cannot record movement with the rapidity of the lens of a camera. The artist realizes this, and presents instead a

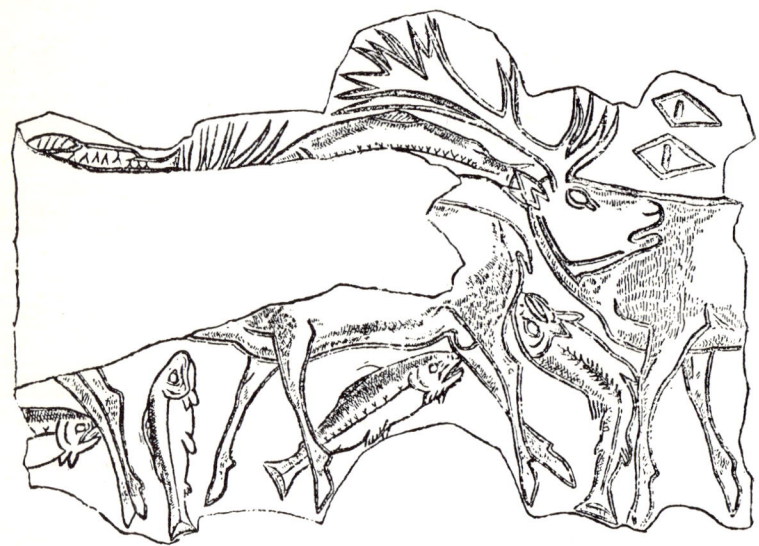

63   Deer crossing a stream. Engraved on a round bone

ENGRAVINGS AND SKETCH-BOOKS

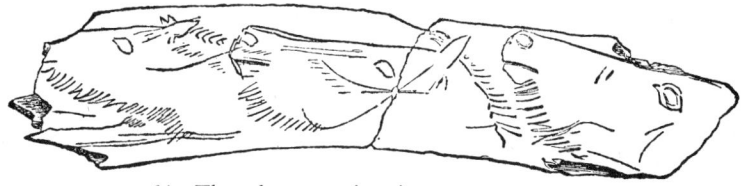

64 Three horses swimming across a stream. Engraved on a flat rib-bone

convention, or design, which we find more real than the reality of the photograph.

Remember that all the engraving and carving was done with flint implements. The engravings illustrated show deer walking across a river, and also horses' heads, drawn as if they were swimming across another river. You can see the last engraving at the British Museum, and also many others. The stone block in fig. 65 is an artist's sketch-book with a beautifully drawn bison on it. This is also at the British Museum.

The drawings and engravings convince us that the artists knew the animals, and that their work was actual life-drawing; in this way we can find that among the Madeleine animals were mammoth, reindeer, and the great Irish deer, the bison and horse, the musk ox, glutton, and Arctic hare. These show that the climate was for some part of the Madeleine Period colder than in Aurignac times.

The illustrations we have given are sufficient to prove that the Madeleine people were a very highly gifted race. These people were becoming civilized, and they were artists, and so would have been pleasant and friendly. We cannot say how they said "How do you do?" to one another; perhaps like the New Zealanders they rubbed noses. Darwin when he went there wrote: "they then squatted themselves down and held up their faces; my companion standing over them, placed the bridge of his nose at right angles to

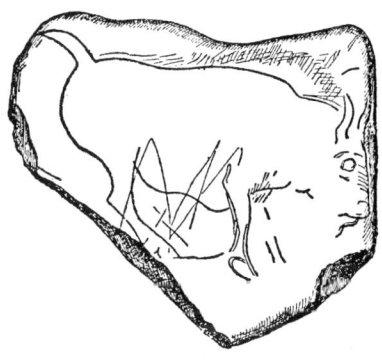

65 A Magdalenian artist's sketch-book

theirs, and commenced pressing. This lasted rather longer than a cordial shake of the hand with us; and as we vary the force of the grasp of the hand in shaking, so they do in pressing. During the process they uttered comfortable little grunts."

To sum up, if it is correct that certain bone rods which have been found at Aurignac stations in France are the bows of bow-drills (*41*), then this must be noted as another very considerable step forward. It is obvious that the Aurignac men must have had some ready method for drilling their shaft-straighteners (*40*). The bow-drill led to the modern lathe. We shall see that in later times the people knew how to turn quite well, and it is probable that they used a type of the primitive pole lathe. In this the rotary movement was conveyed to the article to be turned by a rope which was passed around it in the same way that the bowstring was applied to the drill to turn it. The potter's wheel, which again follows later on, is descended from the bow-drill.

At the end of the third chapter we suggested that man, at first only concerned with food, had begun to realize that there was a spiritual side to his nature. In Madeleine times we find the manifestations of this in an appreciation of beauty; there were artists in those days.

Now Art is a much maligned word; it really means *doing* things, whereas science is *knowing* things. People nowadays think of an artist as a painter; we should like to define that individual as any man, or woman, who puts more into a job of work than they expect to take out of it. An engineer may be a very good artist. A fine motor-car is a work of Art; it has Beauty of form, and is designed with Truth, or it would not do its job, so that it possesses two of the great qualities; there remains only Goodness. It therefore follows that no man can do fine work unless he has some appreciation of the underlying principles on which humanity has built itself up. At the very worst he can only be one-third bad, so credit must be given to the artists of all kinds.

We like to think that good work has been one of the prime factors in the civilization of man, and we believe that dull mechanical work destroys the brain.

We wonder, when our turn comes to be dug up and have our skulls measured, say in A.D. 5000, if the archaeologists of that

66 A Palaeolithic Rock Shelter
After Movius

67 A Neolithic Religious Sanctuary at Avebury
Crown Copyright

ART AND SCIENCE

far-away tomorrow will say, Here was a people who threw away their heritage, and arrested their development, because they lost the use of their hands.

But so far as our friends the Madeleine men are concerned, judged by their work they had made great advances, and, like the Eskimo who so closely resembles them, must have been a pleasant people.

Chapter V

THE MESOLITHIC PERIOD OR THE END OF THE OLD STONE AGE

AT the end of the last Ice Age, when the weather began to get warmer, the herds of horses and reindeer followed the ice northwards towards the Polar region and many of the Madeleine men may have followed them. Those who remained behind in England and France are known by other names, but are probably the descendants of the Madeleine men and other known tribes from nearby regions. Most of these peoples can be recognized by their small flint arrow-heads or microliths. These are chisel-shaped arrow-heads used for killing small birds and animals. The first people we know anything about in France after the disappearance of the Madeleine men are those named after the Cave of Mas d'Azil near Toulouse. The Mas d'Azil men, like all these early peoples, were widely distributed, and traces of their handiwork have been found as far apart as the cave of Mas d'Azil, Ariège, near Lourdes, in the south of France, and Oban in Scotland. The Scottish discoveries of harpoons are very interesting. They show that the ice was retreating, and man was making his way into the tracts of the newly uncovered land.

We know what these men were like because they had a curious habit of removing the heads from the bodies of their dead and burying the skulls like eggs in nests. At the Ofnet Cave, near Nördlingen, Bavaria, South Germany, twenty-seven were found together buried in red ochre. This would suggest that the Mas d'Azil men used to paint their bodies in their lifetime, and so the colour was buried with them for use in the spirit world. One skull of a small child had many shells placed near it—perhaps as playthings. Round another was a chaplet of deer's teeth, and all were placed in the same way, looking westward. The actual bodies were probably consumed by fire; later cremation was a usual method, the ashes being buried in an urn.

Here is a new fact; most of the old races we have been writing

AZILIAN MAN

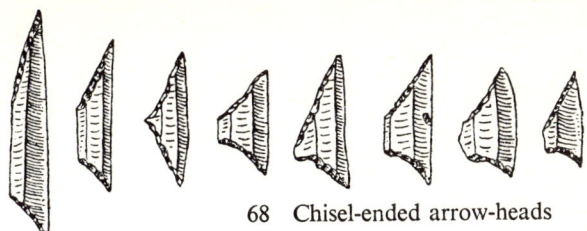

68   Chisel-ended arrow-heads

about were long-headed (dolichocephalic); we now find side by side with this type, brachycephalic, or a rounder-headed people. The fact that individuals of the two races were buried in the same grave points to their having lived together happily. So that if some Madeleine people moved north after the mammoth and the reindeer, others remained behind.

We do not find any beautiful paintings in this period. Man was beginning to look on animals from a different point of view. In the old days he had the hunter's eye, quick to note beauty of body and grace of movement, which he expressed in drawings; in Mas d'Azil days he may have begun to look on himself as a herdsman, though so far only the dog was domesticated. The climate was milder, with westerly winds and warm rains; the waters were rising. Great Britain was an island, and great forests spread over the land, except where the Loess lay thick (p. 32), and by its fineness prevented the trees from taking root. Man, who had been free to roam over the tundra, was now hemmed in, so the old nomadic life passed away, and he began to have possessions.

These had to be useful, and we do not find any cunning work in ivory. The awl takes the place of the needle. Flint is revived for making implements, but in a rougher way than those of Solutré times. Stag horn is used for harpoons instead of reindeer horn, so the Mas d'Azil men also were fishermen.

The most interesting things which they have

69   Mas d'Azil painted pebbles

THE MESOLITHIC PERIOD

left behind them are the painted stones found at Mas d'Azil. These are flattish in shape, about 2 inches across, and painted with signs (*69*). Some of them are surprisingly like early forms of letters—red and black were used. The use to which these stones were put is unknown, but they may have been tallies or accounts. If today you ask a labouring man to cart bricks or tiles, and keep count, he will do so in tens. These he chalks up on the barn door, and obtains his hundreds by ten tens. So these stones may have been tokens or tallies used by Mas d'Azil man in keeping the accounts of his trade by barter. We can be quite sure that some sort of trade had been in existence even long before this time. In Upper Palaeolithic times cowrie shells were found with the Crô-Magnon type of skeleton at Laugerie-Basse. Four were near the head, and two at each elbow, knee, and foot. They must have been sewn on the clothing. These would have come from the Mediterranean, and would have been rarities in the centre of France. The chiefs would have desired them on the principle that fine feathers, or shells, make fine birds, or men. So, perhaps, skins or harpoons were given in exchange. The exchange of commodities still remains as the basis of our trade, and we use money or bills of exchange as tallies or tokens. Life was becoming easier, and was perhaps not so much of a desperate struggle for survival as it had been.

The Glacial Period had receded into the past, and the climate was temperate. Whereas in Madeleine times the countryside had the appearance of the Arctic tundra where the Eskimo now live, in Mas d'Azil times it became well wooded.

Hunting tribes like the Mas d'Azil men are known from England and Spain and also from Scandinavia where they are the first inhabitants. During the Ice Ages Scandinavia was, of course, entirely covered with ice. Around the shores of the Mediterranean hunting was still good, and paintings on rocks are known from this period. Some of them are just as beautiful as those painted by Madeleine man. Those we illustrate show a deer hunt (*70*), a man chasing two stags (*71*), and a woman gathering honey from a bees'-nest. The man seems to be wearing garters and feathers in his hair, and the woman has her hair worn in a long bob. From the south of France we also have an engraving of an ibex, but this is drawn in quite a different style with a single line, and is not so lifelike as the older drawings.

THE OBAN DEPOSITS

The probable Mas d'Azil deposits at Oban were found in a cave opening on to a sea beach. On the rocky floor of the cave were successive deposits: first a pebbly gravel washed in by high tides, then a bed of shells, then gravel, and on top of this another shell-bed with a final topping of black earth, formed in later ages. The level of the land has gone up, perhaps as it lost its tremendous load of ice, or that of the sea gone down, because the cave is now some 30 feet above the sea-level.

70 A deer hunt

THE MESOLITHIC PERIOD

71   A man chasing two stags

In the shell-beds are shells of oysters, limpets, whelks, the claws of lobsters, the bones of large sea fish, red deer, goat, pig, and many other animals. Ashes remain where the cooking hearths were. From all these remains we can be quite sure that Mas d'Azil man was both fisherman and hunter, and the bones of the large sea fish mean that he took his harpoon to sea, in some form of canoe, or boat, covered with skins. Man about this time seems to have been drawn more and more to the water.

Most of the Mesolithic remains in Denmark are found in what are called Kitchen Middens. A midden is a rubbish heap, and these mounds are sometimes 100 yards long by 50 wide by 1 high, and were formed of the refuse of the meals and life of prehistoric man. They are labelled there with the splendid name of *Kjökkenmöddinger*, and are largely formed of oyster shells, with the bones of stag, roe-deer, and wild boar. The long bones have been cracked to extract the marrow. The people do not appear to have grown any crops, or domesticated any animals, except the dog, so they had not made any great advances on the civilization of the Old Stone Age. It was the pleasant loafing life of the beach-comber. The sea when it is angry casts up all kinds of edible flotsam, and in kindlier mood at low tide man could hunt over the rocks, as we do today during our summer holidays, and find lobster and crab, oyster and mussel, prawns and shrimps, and the humble winkle.

THE LAST HUNTERS

We find the remains of similar people, and their shell heaps, in different parts of the British Isles. These people possessed dug-out canoes, or skin-covered boats, with which to go fishing, and used harpoons like the Old Stone Age men. It may be that, as their flint implements were rough and not very effective, they were forced to the seaside by the encroaching forests. As the weather improved, after the Ice Ages, the trees grew, and man could not as yet make sufficient clearings in which to start agriculture.

The evidence that we can gain points to this dim beginning of the Mesolithic Period, some 10,000 to 12,000 years ago, as a time when the world was gathering its forces. The Old Stone Age culminated in the wonderful flint work of Solutré, and the La Madeleine paintings; after that came decline. The old hunters followed in the track of the Mammoth and the Reindeer, and reached northern latitudes, where their successors of today, the Eskimo, live. They left behind them other tribes of hunters who were able to adapt themselves to the very

72   A woman gathering honey

THE MESOLITHIC PERIOD

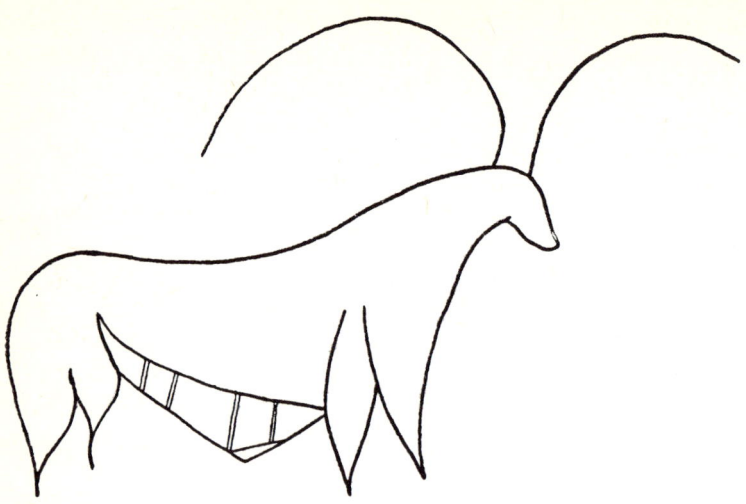

73 Wall painting of an ibex

different condition of life along the sea-coasts and in the newly grown forests of post-ice-age Europe.

Then wise men came out of the East, and later we shall try to show how we in England were affected by these migrations. There were kings in Egypt as early as 4500 B.C., and the Mediterranean, which had seen the Crô-Magnon, and Grimaldi men, in the Old Stone Age, was to see these others who, coming from the East, or South-East, in the New Stone Age, were to press along to the cry of "Westward Ho!", and build up new civilizations.

Whether the midden people died out, or were stimulated by these new-comers we cannot be sure. They had domesticated the dog, and it may have occurred to them to do the same with other animals, and so save themselves the trouble of hunting.

This we find is the next step; man became a herdsman, and had flocks to tend. This added to his responsibilities; while as hunter, or beach-comber, his cares were few, he must have found that with possessions his troubles began. It was necessary to find pasture for the little flock, and in the winter, no matter how hard the times were, he must keep alive some few to carry on the strain; the animals needed guarding at night; better pots and

ENGLAND IN NEOLITHIC TIMES

pans were necessary for storing milk, and in a hundred ways he was moved to bestir and adapt himself to the new conditions which arose out of becoming a man of property.

We will now turn to the geographical conditions which confronted Neolithic man in England, and the bearing which these had on his mode of living, and the necessity that he was under of finding pasture for his flocks.

In the Old Stone Age, men walked across dry land where the Straits of Dover are now (*see* p. 32); but as the waters rose after the last Ice Age, the isthmus across got smaller and smaller, until England was completely severed. It is probable that this did not occur until some time after the beginning of the New Stone Age, and even then the Channel would not have been so wide as it is now. This was, and still is, the great Gate into England; here have passed men of the Old and New Stone Ages, Goidels, Brythons, Belgae and Romans, Saxons, Danes, and Normans. There have been, and are today, other routes, but none that can compare with the southern end of Watling Street.

We want our readers to bear in mind the physical characteristics of England; its shape; its mountains and rivers; where the watersheds and the marshy ground. Readers will remember that constant alteration has brought it to its present shape. Thanet has been an island, and the Lympne Flats under water. The Wash and Fens were unreclaimed, and the East Coast by Dunwich has been steadily eaten away; there have been alterations along the South Coast and by the Isle of Wight.

In the early Neolithic days, men could stand in Gaul and look across to Kent, and say, "There is another land there like our own; there also can we walk dry foot on the hills, and find pasture for our beasts. The grass is growing brown here, let us go and see what the country is like."

A drought in these early days would have led to great migrations, and the pressure from behind has forced the men on the coast to make the great adventure. The Old

74 Danish midden axe

THE MESOLITHIC PERIOD

Testament contains the finest pictures of nomadic herdsmen. In Genesis xiii, we read how Abraham and Lot returned out of Egypt, and there was strife between their herdsmen, because the land was not able to bear them, and Abraham said to Lot, "Is not the whole land before thee? Separate thyself, I pray thee, from me: if thou wilt take the left hand, then I will go to the right."

Chapter VI

THE NEW STONE AGE

THE New Stone Age or the Neolithic Period is recognized as the period when the first farmers arrived in England. They came on a long journey travelling very slowly for hundreds of years from the countries in the Near East where farming was first invented.

When the first Neolithic men arrived here, they would have found excellent pasture then, as now, on the Downs, and flint for their tools. They would move along the line of the old road later called the Pilgrims' Way, on the escarpment of the North Downs, secure from wolf or man. We find today traces of Neolithic man on this road; there is Kitscoty to the north-west of Maidstone; the Coldrum monument to the west on the other side of the Medway; the pit-dwellings in Rose Wood near Ightham—all dating from the New Stone Age. Neolithic man introduced sheep, goats, pigs, and cattle (*Bos longifrons*), like the small black Welsh cattle. These necessitated enclosures; so we find along the trackways on the Downs and on Salisbury Plain earthworks where cattle could be herded together for safe keeping or for slaughter.

These camps are only found in the South of England; for not only was pasture better on the Downs, but there were fewer trees. The country was far more wooded than it is now, and man had not as yet the implements with which to make extensive clearings in the forests. It is a mistake, however, to think of these as dense tropical jungles, because the climate then was temperate, as it is now. The undrained country would have been a more formidable obstacle than the forests, and places like the Sussex Weald which was all sticky clay. The forests were full of wild animals; there was the Irish elk and the wild ox (aurochs), bears and beavers, wild cats and red deer, wild boars and the wolf, and Neolithic man hunted these with dogs.

Later and more adventurous immigrants seem to have coasted round until they came to the chalk at Eastbourne. They

75　Dug-out canoe

would have set out in their dug-out canoes(75), and some of these have been found as long as 50 feet. On the South Downs again are earthworks and tumuli, linked up by trackways leading to Stonehenge. Others came in at the Wash, which in those days extended inland much farther than it does today, and here Icknield Way goes south to the Goring Gap on the Thames, and then by way of the Berkshire Downs again to Stonehenge. Later on Maiden Castle, near Dorchester, and its connection with the trackways, points to traffic and trade by sea. The range of Neolithic man seems to have been the Downs, the Blackdown Hills to Devon and Cornwall, the Mendips, the Cotswolds to the Northampton Heights, the South Pennines and Lincolnshire Hills, the Yorkshire Wolds and Moors, and the Glamorgan Hills, and the north and west of Scotland, and all these parts are connected by trackways which converge on Salisbury Plain and Stonehenge, which appears to have been the richest part of England in the Neolithic and Bronze Ages, and the seat of such spiritual and civil government as there was.

It should be noted that the trackways follow the watersheds, and so avoid the crossing of rivers—a serious obstacle to flocks and herds. In later days the great river valleys formed avenues of approach for immigrants into the country, and the fact that so many of these are on the East Coast, has rendered us peculiarly liable to invasion on that side. The tide runs up the Humber and Ouse nearly to York; up the Trent to just beyond Gainsborough, and the Thames to Teddington.

NEOLITHIC GEOGRAPHY

Archaeologists cannot prove how many of these trackways were in use in Neolithic times, for Neolithic settlements and monuments are rare by comparison with those of the later prehistoric Ages. For the Bronze Age we have a great many of these monuments, and these can plainly be seen, especially in the south of England, strung out along the trackways, where these still exist and have not been destroyed by later ploughing—for example, on the Downs and the Salisbury Plain. We may be certain, however, that Neolithic man used the trackways or others very like them—when he moved by land and with cattle—because in heavily forested country it always pays to choose the well-drained land when you move from place to place.

In this earliest period of England's settlement by agricultural peoples—by farmers and herdsmen—we should think of people moving around at two very different speeds. First there were the explorers, the discovers of new land, and the earliest traders, or groups of farmers who still did a considerable amount of hunting. These groups travelled far and wide by the rivers and trackways, and quite fast—even by modern standards. Then there were the tribes or large families engaged in planting corn and looking after cattle—these cleared patches of forest, near where they landed on the English coast, and only moved on two or three miles at a time, every two or three years, when they had exhausted the food for their cattle, or the possibility of growing corn in their woodland clearing. These groups took hundreds of years to cover England.

Before we examine the works of Neolithic man in more detail, it will be as well to try and find out something about him and the European Races during the Neolithic, Bronze, and Early Iron Ages. We can refer to ourselves as Anglo-Saxons or Britons, and yet be very wide of the mark. Assuming that we were cruising over Great Britain in an aeroplane, we could in a few days cover the length and breadth of the land, and if we kept our eyes open when we landed, we should find very varying types in our own country.

In parts of Essex, and the South Midlands and Chilterns; on the hills to the west of the Severn in Worcestershire, Shropshire, and Herefordshire; in Romney Marsh, the Weald, and the Isle of Ely, we should find a large proportion of dark-haired people with long heads, and the explanation of this is, that as these parts were off the main lines of Saxon immigration, the old British blood has lingered on. The Saxons penetrated into the country on the line of the Thames, and this element is strong in Berkshire, Oxfordshire, Hampshire, Sussex, and up the Thames Valley to the Cotswolds; here you will find fair people with blue eyes. In Leicestershire and Lincolnshire are Danish types with long faces, and heads rather high behind; high cheek-bones, and well-formed noses; they appear to have driven the Anglians to the Derbyshire hills in olden days. In Yorkshire we find a typically English people; shrewd, vigorous, and obstinate; successful in business; hard-headed and practical, yet with a great love of music. In the Shetlands, Orkneys, Hebrides, and parts of Caithness are splendid men of Norwegian descent. In the Highlands a Gaelic stock, quick-tempered and emotional; in the Lowlands, and the eastern coast-lands, a frugal hard-working people descended from Angles, Danes, and immigrants from the east.

It is obvious, then, that our own island provides us with some very fair samples of the European races, and if we are to understand our own history, or discover where these types have come from, we must cross to the mainland.

The European Races have been divided into three large families or groups, the Nordic, Alpine, and Mediterranean, and the history of Europe is a recital of the migrations and minglings of these types. Nordic means Northern, and this type is sometimes called Teutonic; these people came from the steppe region to the north of the mountains between Europe and Asia. As the climate improved after the last Ice Age this became forest. The people were tall and strong-boned, with fair hair, and blue eyes, and they were long-headed.

The Alpine people came from the mountain zone of Europe; they were thick-set, and round-headed.

The Mediterranean men came from the coast-lands of that sea; they were dark, long-headed, with oval faces and aquiline noses; of middle height, not more than 5 feet 6 inches, and the women shorter and not very robust.

The Nordic and Mediterranean types were probably descendants of the later long-headed people of the Old Stone Age, and the Alpine later arrivals from the east.

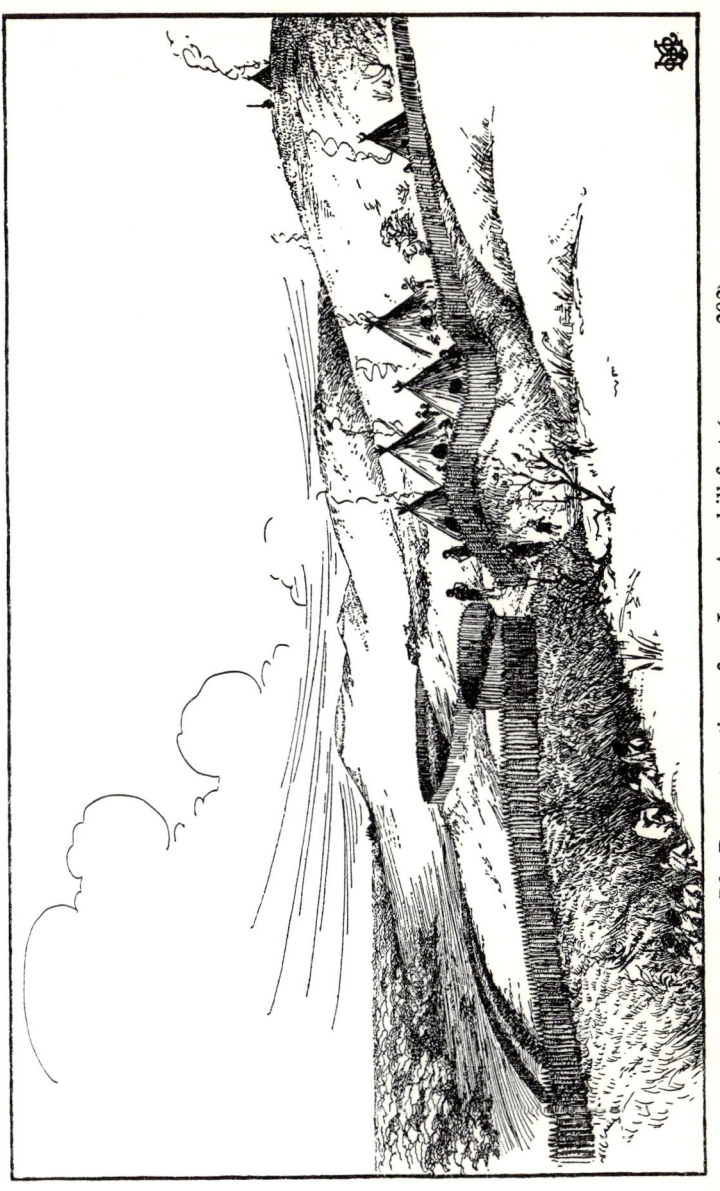

76 Reconstruction of an Iron Age hill fort (*see page 202*)

THE NEW STONE AGE

It is to the Mediterranean stock that we must look for the first of the Neolithic people in this country. It is thought that working along the coast-lands of the western part of the Mediterranean they struck up through the Carcassone Gap between the Pyrenees and the Cevennes, and thence through the west of France until they came to Brittany and Normandy, then worked along the coast until they came to where the Straits of Dover now are. Remember this was not done in a day, or many days, but was a movement lasting for hundreds of years.

The later Mediterranean people were the builders of the Megalithic monuments; the menhirs, dolmens, and chambered barrows which culminated in Stonehenge, and spread from the Eastern Mediterranean across to Western Europe and our own land. Megalithic is derived from two Greek words, *megas*, great, and *lithos*, stone, and its most distinctive contribution to the art of building was the evolution of the lintel; in this detail it was allied to Egyptian and Greek building. Stonehenge is the triumph of the lintel, and the main building that we know so well is believed to date from the earlier part of the Bronze Age.

These dolmen builders may have retreated before the round-headed Bronze Age men, who seem to have come from the Eastern Mediterranean, through Gaul to Britain. They were stalwart, dark, broad-headed men, and arrived here about 1800 B.C. It is thought that these earliest round-heads were not Goidels, and we will explain this later. It is quite possible that they may have had something to do with megalithic building, as they associated with the Neolithic long-heads; we know this, because in the round barrows, which are of Bronze Age, round- and long-heads are found buried together. The Bronze men brought with them their flat bronze axes (*106*), and if at the first they could not manufacture these they did obtain them by trade.

About the same time the "Beaker" people arrived on the north and east coasts. They are called "Beaker" people because of a pottery vessel found in their graves (*125*, 1). It may not have been a drinking-cup or beaker, but it looks like one. They may have come from Spain or from Germany where their pottery is equally common. These Beaker men were a mixture of Alpine and Nordic, combining the broad heads of the Alpine with the

77 Neolithic Weaving Pattern from the Swiss Lakes

78 Bronze Age Face Ornament

79 A Gold Breastplate of the Bronze Age
After Hope-Taylor

LATER PREHISTORIC RACES

fair colouring, strength and length of bone of the Nordic. They were tall and strong-browed.

About this time we are able to find out that the conditions of life were becoming easier. The people lived longer lives, they were bigger than in Neolithic times, and there was less difference between the size of men and women.

At a later day, perhaps about 700 to 500 B.C., the first of the Celts arrived; they were an Aryan-speaking people who burned their dead. Here we might explain what is meant by the Aryan-speaking peoples, because the spread of this language is one of the wonderful things in the world's history, like the La Madeleine painting. The Aryan language is also described as being Indo-European, Indo-Iranian, and Indo-Germanic. Towards the end of the eighteenth century, similarities were noticed in the construction of languages seemingly so different as Sanscrit, Greek, Latin, German, and Celtic, and later all the European languages, except Turkish, Finnish, and one or two others, were added, with some modern Indian languages, to a group which has been derived from this primitive Aryan tongue. This does not mean that all the millions of Aryan-speaking people today are descended from Aryan stock; it does point to some wonderful idea which spread across Europe like a flame burning dry grass.

The exact spot where the original Aryans lived is still a matter of debate: one idea is that it was in south Russia or Hungary; another, on the Iranian plateau to the south-east of the Caspian Sea. From there the language spread south-east across the Indus into India. The route to Europe may have been to the east of the Caspian Sea and then west across the Volga, Don, and Dnieper, whence came the Beaker people. Or north-west from the Iranian plateau, and south of the Black Sea into Asia Minor and the Ægean. Now language does not spread as a fashion, but because it is the vehicle of thought embodying a dominating idea.

The diffusion of the Aryan language coincided with great changes and migrations of the European peoples. The old Neolithic civilization had carried men forward as a tribe, and in a state which did not offer much opportunity to the individual. While the pioneer work was being done, the adventurous men had plenty to occupy them, and then may have become restless as conditions became more settled, and have seized power, not

THE NEW STONE AGE

necessarily from a selfish point of view, but to satisfy wider ambitions and to obtain more movement and colour in life. We come to the Age of Heroes. The chieftain, or patriarch of the tribe, has to give way to the hero, who welds it into a nation and becomes a king.

The Celts, an Aryan-speaking, fair-haired people began to come over from the Continent about 500 B.C. bringing with them the first weapons and implements of iron. They spoke two kindred but slightly differing tongues which still persist in these islands in forms which, in the main, are not greatly altered. They were called, according to this division of speech, the Goidels and Brythons, and by Roman writers the Gauls and Britons. The descendants of the former are the Irish, the Highlanders of Scotland, and the Manx, of the latter the Welsh and the Cornish.

About 75 B.C. came the Belgae, of Celtic stock with an admixture of Germanic, and Caesar found them in the possession of south-east Britain when he arrived.

Having now given an outline sketch of the various peoples we shall meet with, we will go back to the first of these, the men of the New Stone Age. We will examine first their implements, and then later consider the work they did with these tools. These Neolithic implements are not necessarily of polished stone, as some people seem to think. Flint was still chipped as in the Old Stone Age: sometimes it was chipped and ground, or polished in parts; sometimes completely so.

At Cissbury near Worthing, and Grime's Graves near Weeting in Norfolk, the pits formed by the early miners to obtain their flints have been discovered, and it is thought the implements were roughly finished here for export. They used deer-horn picks, and shoulder-blades as shovels. These can be seen in the Prehistoric Room at the British Museum. Fig. *80* shows the miners using these deer-horn picks like you use a modern pick, but often the flint was too solid to be broken out of the chalk in this way. So the miners hammered the point of their pick into a crack in the flint and then used the long handle to lever out a flint block. The springy deer horn or antler was better than anything else could be for this purpose. If you examine these picks carefully you will see the marks where

NEOLITHIC FLINT MINES

someone has hammered hard on the broadest part of the pick with a stone hammer, and lines of small holes have been found around the flint in these ancient mines. This is where someone had started to break out a piece of flint and had never come back to lever it out. The archaeologists who excavated at Grime's Graves in Norfolk actually found the fingerprint of a Neolithic flint miner on one of these deer-horn picks.

Fig. *81* shows a few typical implements, and the way they were hafted or had handles fitted. A is the celt, or axe, and is the Neolithic descendant of the hand-axe of the Old Stone Age. Celts have been found varying from an inch or so long up to 15 inches or 16 inches, and were the most important implements

80 Flint miners

THE NEW STONE AGE

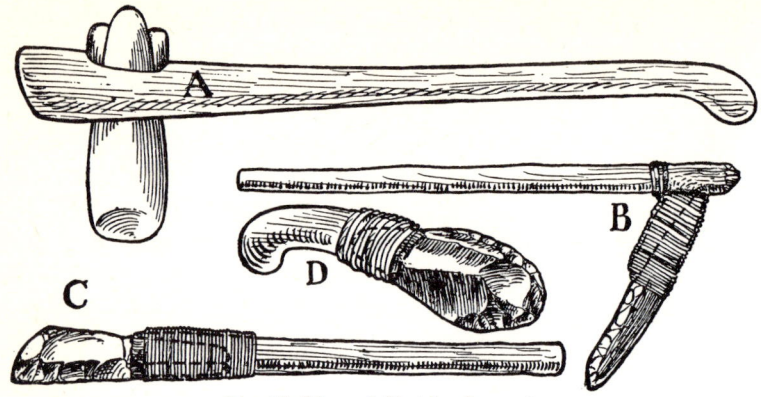

81 Hafting of flint implements

of Neolithic man. They were driven into the head of a wooden handle as at A, and then wedged from the top. Sometimes the celt was fixed into a deer-horn socket driven into the wood. With celts trees were cut down and all the rough carpentry done. The stone celt or axe was the forerunner of the bronze axe, and led to the iron axe which has been one of the most useful tools of man throughout the ages. Fig. *81* A shows a polished stone celt. These at first were chipped out of flint. Then the cutting edge was ground, and finally the whole celt polished. Fig. *81* B shows a rougher, unpolished type, hafted at right angles to the handle for use as an adze; this may have been used like a hoe to chop towards the foot, and must have been very useful in making dug-out canoes. Rougher stones mounted in this way were used perhaps as hoes for agriculture. For this method of hafting any branched stick could be used, and the flint bound on with rawhide thongs. Fig. *81* C shows how a chisel-shaped flake could be mounted, and D a scraper. Scrapers were as useful and general in the New,

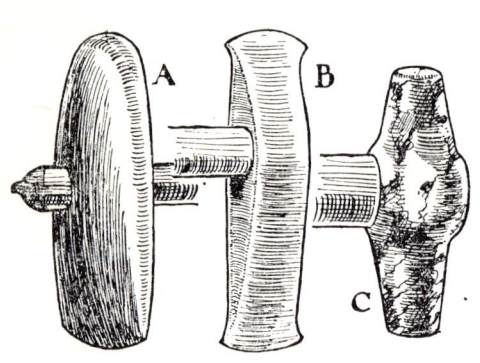

82 Stone axes and hammers

FLINT AND STONE TOOLS

as in the Old Stone Age, and probably served to remove the fat from skins and to scrape wood. A very usual shape was that of an oyster-shell; the Eskimo use these, and mount them in ivory handles, and their flaying knives are like the thin oval flakes of greenstone, found in Scotland, and called Picts' knives. Fig. *82* A shows a polished stone celt hafted at right angles for use as an adze. B is a stone axe with double edge, and C a stone hammer. In thinking of how these were made we must remember the extraordinary patience of the savage.

The Neolithic implement maker used volcanic rocks for his axes, and after roughly trimming these to shape, finished by grinding the axe on a grindstone—not one that runs round, but by rubbing the axe on a stone, as the carpenter sharpens his plane iron. The boring of the hole was done last, with a stick, or hollow bone, and sand and water. Any sand hard enough to scratch the stone would cut the hole in time. The drill could have been turned with a bow (*41*). Odysseus drills out the eye of Polyphemus by means of a stake with a leather thong around it, "as when a man bores a ship's timber".

Some of the stone axes have one edge and a rounded head, and may have been used for splitting wood, by hammering the head with a wooden mallet. Others have a purposely blunted edge, as if for use as battle-axes, with less chance of cutting the wielder, and just as much power to damage the enemy. Amusing traditions have gathered around the old stone celts; the country people in the past thought they were thunderbolts. Stone hammers were known in Scotland, until the end of the eighteenth century, as Purgatory Hammers, and were supposed to have been buried with the dead, so that they could hammer on the gates of Purgatory, till the heavenly janitor appeared. Another point to be remembered, and one which we have so often emphasized, is that stone continued to be used after the advent of bronze. Sir William Wilde stated in the middle of the nineteenth century that stone hammers and anvils were used by Irish smiths and tinkers until about that time. Again, Sir John Evans, in *Ancient Stone Implements*, published in 1872, says that up till that time flints were sold in country shops for use with steel to make fire. Leaving the larger implements, we can turn to the lance, javelin, and arrow-heads, and the many things which were made out of the flakes. Long flakes up to 8 and 9 inches

THE NEW STONE AGE

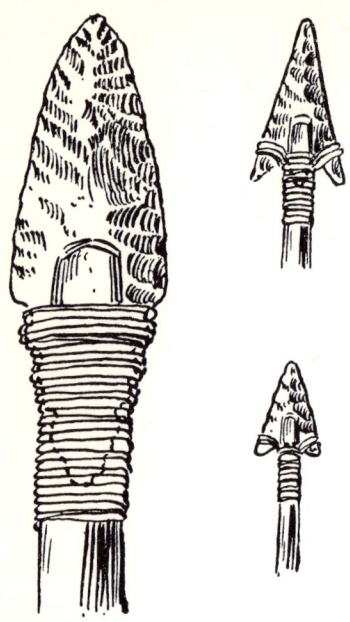

83 Flint spear- and arrow-heads

were possible, and these were used for lance-heads; shorter ones for javelins and arrows; thicker and rougher flakes for scrapers. Having obtained the flakes, the maker then proceeded to trim these into the desired shape, by what the archaeologists call secondary flaking. In some of the Danish specimens the flaking is rippled along the edge of the implement in a most delightful way. Opinions are divided as to how this secondary flaking was done. However, it is all done by some form of pressure flaking which we saw was invented in the Upper Palaeolithic. A flint punch, or fabricator, may have been used; or the flake held flat, face uppermost on an anvil stone, may have been trimmed by hammering tiny flakes off the edge with a hammer-stone. The Eskimo place the flake over a slight hollow in a log, and then press an ivory tool which spalls off small flakes. Captain John Smith, writing in 1606 of the Indians of Virginia, said: "His arrow-head he maketh quickly with a little bone, which he ever weareth at his bracert (guard on wrist against bow-string), of any splint of stone or glasse in the form of a heart, and these they glew to the end of their arrowes. With the sinewes of deer and the tops of deer's horns boiled to a jelly, they make a glew which will not dissolve in water." This means a form of mounting as fig. *83*. The arrow-heads must have called for wonderful handling when being made. As with the axes, tradition has gathered round the arrow-heads, which, until quite recent times, were called elf-darts by the country people, who thought that the fairies used them to injure cattle.

Having seen something of the tools which Neolithic man possessed, we can pass on to the work he did with these, and will begin with the houses he built. In fig. *76* very simple huts

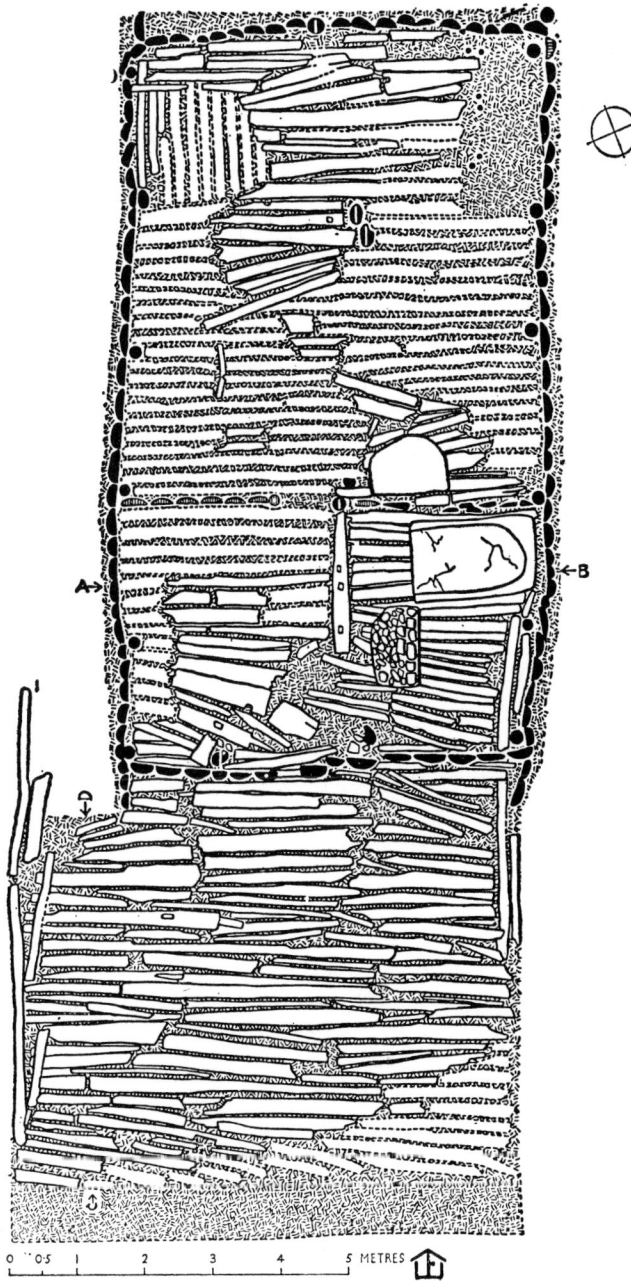

84 Plan of a Neolithic house at Aichbuhl

THE NEW STONE AGE

85   Aichbuhl Neolithic village

are shown which resemble those of the Old Stone Age shown in fig. 57.

These huts are round and seem to have been used both in England and France during the Neolithic times and also in some of the countries in the Mediterranean. The best British houses of this type were found by accident under the sands at Skara Brae and Rinyo in the Orkney Islands, off the Scottish coast. These islands are quite bare and, as there was no wood to make the houses, they are built of stones. If you go there you can still see the houses, which lead into one another and have stone beds and stone chairs as well as stone fireplaces and stone boxes in which to keep water. Unfortunately very few houses have been found in England. Beneath the earth only one or two holes which once held posts still remain. But at Halden in Devon and also in the Cambridgeshire Fenland enough of these post holes have been found to show that some of the Neolithic houses were

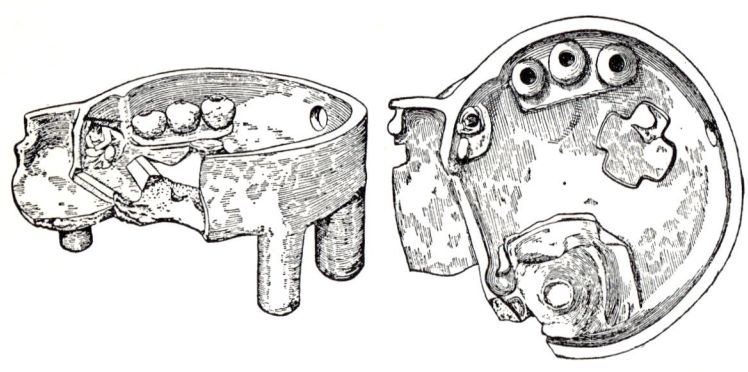

86   A Neolithic dolls' house

NEOLITHIC HOUSES

square or rectangular. We illustrate a good example of this kind of house from Aichbuhl in Germany, where one or two whole villages of this kind of house were discovered. These were preserved in the ground because it had become wet and boggy before the Neolithic men abandoned it, and so the wood had not all rotted away. In the plan of one of these houses (84), you can see that every plank of the floor is still in position.

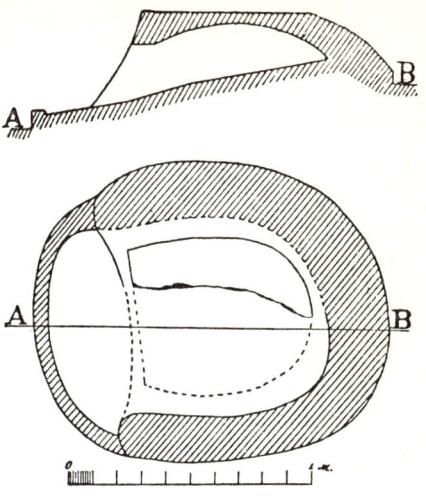

87   Plan of a clay oven

The inside of the house is surrounded by upright wooden planks which were made of logs sawn in half, just like a Canadian log cabin. These are marked on the plan in black. You can see that the house was divided into two rooms, a big one for living in and a small one with a fireplace for cooking. A wall divided these two rooms and if you look carefully you can see the doorway, which has no planks across it. Outside the door of the house is a plank veranda, but there is no outside door visible on the plan. It seems as if there was no way out except by squeezing between the planks. Fig. 85 shows what the excavator thinks a village of these houses must have looked like. Some of this may be guess-work, but there are ways of judging a house's appearance and even its height from a complete excavation of its foundations.

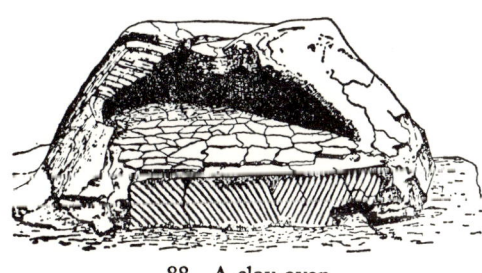

88   A clay oven

Another way we can find out about Neolithic houses is from the house models which some of the Neolithic people made for their children. We illustrate a little house on legs also found in Central

THE NEW STONE AGE

Europe (*86*). This is a little round house with perhaps a mud wall raised off the ground on wooden piles because it was marshy, like the Swiss Neolithic lake villages, or like the Iron Age dwellings at Glastonbury we will be talking about later. In the house you can see three pits for storing grain and water, and a little man grinding grain in one corner. On the other side of the doorway there is a dome-shaped structure with a flat top like a ladies' hat. This can only be seen in the plan of the house model. We only know what this is because we have dug up the real thing in Neolithic houses in this part of the world. It is a clay oven like that seen in fig. *88*.

89 Strike-a-light

We do not know much about the clothes that the men wore who lived in these houses or in those in England.

Flint thumb-scrapers found in the Dartmoor huts suggest skin clothing; though weaving appears to have been started in the Swiss lake dwellings in Neolithic times, it is doubtful if it started here till the Bronze Age. Very few ornaments have been found in long barrows.

Skin clothing does not necessarily mean that Neolithic men only wore the rough pelts of animals; we saw how the women of the Old Stone Age could make very good bone needles, and a visit to the Ethnographical Gallery, at the British Museum,

90 A flint sickle

HOW TO MAKE FIRE

91 Grinding corn

will show us what beautiful skin garments the Eskimo can make. Neolithic garments may not have been quite as well made as these. The Picts, who were descendants of the Neolithic men, tattooed themselves, so this method of decoration may have gone back to the New Stone Age.

Fig. 89 shows a way that the Neolithic woman made fire; a piece of flint was used, in conjunction with a lump of iron pyrites, as a strike-a-light. Pyrites is found in the lower chalk beds, and may first have been used as a hammer-stone on flint, when the resulting sparks would suggest its use as fig. 89. The sparks falling on dry moss could be blown into flame. Very beautiful flint knives (90), have been found and it is thought that these were used as sickles. The reaper

92 Pounding grain

133

THE NEW STONE AGE

gathered the ears of the corn in one hand, and cut these off as shown. When the corn was cut the threshing was a very simple business, and then came the grinding into flour. Fig. *91* shows a saddle-back quern: the grain was placed on this, in the hollow made by use, and the upper stone pushed to and fro until the corn became flour. Neolithic man would hardly have been able to obtain yeast, and probably his bread was unleavened, or the flour mixed with honey and baked into biscuits. Fig. *92* shows a pot quern, like a modern pestle and mortar, which would have been very useful for pounding things up. These querns were made of gritstone.

We come now to one of the most important discoveries of Neolithic man or woman; he or she found out the way to make pottery. The first pots were made without the use of a potter's wheel, probably in the same way that the Kikuyu of Kenya work today. These people temper their clay by pulling it into small pieces and freeing it from stones; it is then dried in the sun, and afterwards mixed with water until it is plastic. A fine sand is then kneaded into it, in the proportion of about half and half, and the clay finished in long rolls. One or two of these are formed into a collar shape, and with one hand inside this, and the other out, it is gradually modelled into the shape of the top half of the pot, more clay being added in rolls as the work proceeds. The half pot is allowed to dry in the sun for some hours, except the lower edge where the join has to come; this is protected by leaves. This edge has rested on leaves while the top half was being made, so that it could be turned more easily, and this movement must later have suggested the potter's wheel. In the next stage this top half is turned upside down on its already finished mouth, on more leaves, and the modelling

93 Making pottery

POT MOULDING

proceeds as before, more material being added as required to form the bottom, the shape being given by one hand in, and the other out, until there is only room for one finger, and then the hole is closed, and the pot finished. Again, a few hours are allowed for hardening, then the pots are placed mouth downwards on the ground, and a bonfire of brushwood made all around them; when this has burned out, and the pots are cool, they are ready for use. The only tool used, beside the hand, is a piece of gourd shell.

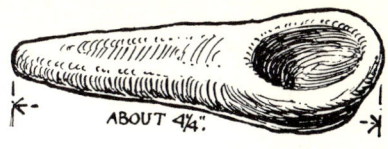

94 Pottery spoon

Fig. 93 shows how Neolithic woman went to work, and fig. 94 a pottery spoon she made, which can be seen at the British Museum.

The Kikuyu pottery is made by women, and the probability is that Neolithic woman did this work, and looked after the home, while her husband was hunter and herdsman. She probably did far more than just cook and mend; we must think of her as an inventor. With pottery the long train was started which has led up to the modern saucepan; before then, meat could only be roasted over a fire, or baked in a cooking-pit, but with a stout earthen pot that could be placed in the ashes the Neolithic equivalent of Irish stew was possible. Water could be heated, and milk and grain stored.

Perhaps it was the woman who noticed that cattle ate the seeds of grasses, and experimented by grinding some between stones; she may have tasted the flour and found it sweet, and then have brought home more seeds. A few seeds blew away into the ground newly turned up at the base of a hut, and the woman watched these growing and watered and tended them. In this way it may have occurred to her to make a garden, and she discovered that cultivation improved the crop; once this fact was appreciated there were endless opportunities; the crab apple, wild plum, and other fruits could be experimented with, and most probably woman was a gardener before man became a farmer; of one thing

THE NEW STONE AGE

we may be quite sure, Neolithic man did not rise up one day and plant an acre of ground without endless experiments and questionings going before.

We have seen something of Neolithic houses and the way Neolithic man lived. He has also left us two types of monument which are still visible on the surface of the ground today. These are his cattle camps and his religious monuments. The cattle camps are the earliest kind of hill enclosure discovered on the Downs. They are just a small area of ground on a low flat hilltop with one, or possibly two, ditches thrown around it. These ditches provide the earth for a small bank just inside them which, when it had stakes set along the top, was sufficient to keep the cattle inside. The ditch was only a quarry for the earth to form this bank and when Neolithic man had sufficient earth he did not bother to dig out the ditch all the way around the hilltop. That is why these camps are called Interrupted Ditch Camps. Sometimes they are called Causeway Camps, because there is a causeway between each section of the ditch that has not been dug out. Archaeologists think that these camps were used when the cattle were rounded up in the autumn to be killed and perhaps salted down. There was little grown in those days, and there was no way to feed the cattle through the autumn, so all the bulls except one would be killed, and perhaps many of the cows too.

We can now pass on to the Neolithic Long Barrow, or Burial mound, because, apart from its spiritual significance, which we will discuss later, it has great interest in its structure. The Long Barrow derives its name from the fact that it is egg-shaped in plan, and there are two types; those having chambers inside for the interment, and others where the bodies were covered directly by the earth; these latter have a ditch at the sides leaving a wide path at the original level at each end. Generally placed east and west, the burial is usually in the east end, which is higher and broader than the west. It is a curious fact that the Neolithic long-head built a long barrow, while that of the later round-headed Bronze man was round.

Chambered long barrows are also built mainly of earth, but in the interior a passage is left, and several small rooms or burial chambers are built usually with very large flat blocks of stone.

LONG BARROWS

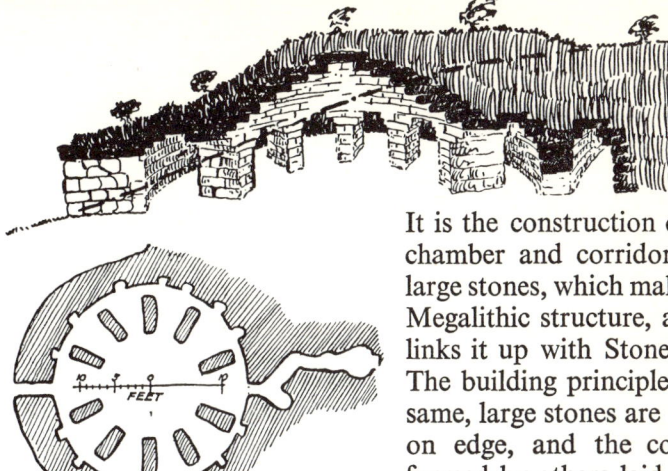

95 Earth house, Usinish, South Uist, Hebrides

It is the construction of this chamber and corridor, with large stones, which makes it a Megalithic structure, and so links it up with Stonehenge. The building principle is the same, large stones are placed on edge, and the covering formed by others laid flat as lintels. In other structures of this sort, where the span was too great for one stone, courses of masonry were projected from either side as corbels, until the central space was narrow enough to be bridged (*see* figs. *95* and *96*). This is the same method of building as that employed in the Tomb of Agamemnon. Around the outside of the barrow came a dry stone wall with upright sarsen stones at intervals. This dry stone walling was a great accomplishment on the part of the builders, and marked an advance. Long-headed skeletons were sometimes found in these chambers and there is no evidence of cremation. These chambered barrows are planned much on the same lines as the Bronze Age Temples of Malta. Sometimes the bones found in the Long Barrows are disjointed, as if they had been placed there some while after death; and it may well be that only the heroes were thought worthy of such burial. Because the barrows were used for more than one burial, it has been suggested that slaves may have been sacrificed to accompany their tribal chiefs to the spirit world, in the same way that implements and pottery were broken, and animals slaughtered, but it is doubtful if slavery was yet possible. We shall probably be quite safe if we regard these barrows as tribal mausoleums, where the people could assemble and hold services. They are a visible sign to us that Neolithic man

THE NEW STONE AGE

believed in a life hereafter, and built them as an emphatic assertion that death is not final. It must have needed some great impulse to bring the tribe together, and make them willing to undertake such a vast work as the construction of a barrow.

This provision of houses for the dead throws an interesting sidelight on the belief of those days; it suggests that in Neolithic times the spirit was tied to the earth for some little while, whereas in the later Bronze Age burials, when the body was burned, it seems as if the spirit was freed at once to go to the spirit-world. The homes for the dead may have been modelled on those of living men; there is a range of habitations which would appear to have been developments of this idea. Figs. *95* and *96* show what are known as Picts' Houses in Scotland, and this form of stone construction covered with earth is clearly derived from the chambered barrows. Again, the Eskimo houses (*97, 98*) seem to be survivals carried to the north. In fig. *97* there is a long tunnel entrance leading to the hut, with the beds at A, and the cooking-places at B. The roof of the hut is formed of skins, with a layer of moss between, carried on the poles shown in the sketch. The window is of membrane stretched between whales' jaw bones. The snow house (*98*) is of the same form. There are Picts' houses in Scotland which consist of a paved trench lined with masonry, and covered with stone slabs which terminate in a round chamber.

Fig. *99* shows a Picts' Tower, Doon, or Broch, of a type found in Sutherland, Caithness, Orkneys, Shetlands, and the Hebrides. The little door shown is only 3 feet 8 inches high, by 3 feet broad, and leads through the wall, which is 10 feet 6 inches thick, with a guard cell off the passage 4 feet high and 9 feet long, with a doorway 2 feet square. There is a circular court inside, open to

96 Picts house, Sutherland
(Iron Age)

138

MEGALITHS AND ROCK HOUSES

97   Eskimo rock hut

the sky, and in the wall of this, opposite the entrance, another door leads to a passage winding up in the thickness of the wall to upper galleries, all of which are very low, and lighted by windows into the inner court. It is very difficult to date such buildings, but these Picts' towers are Megalithic in character, and built of dry stone; in design they are first cousins to the Nuraghi of Sardinia, which are fortified dwellings. The Picts are supposed to have descended from the Neolithic stock, and, it may well be, built these towers, perhaps as late as Roman times, in this distant part of the country. And as we have seen, though the earliest Megalithic monuments are built in the Neolithic Period in Britain, this method of building was still in use in the Bronze Age.

Fig. *100* shows a Cromlech or Dolmen; this was part of the chamber of a barrow, from which the encircling earth has been

98   Eskimo snow house

THE NEW STONE AGE

99 Picts' tower (Iron Age)

removed, and ploughed away. Its construction is as described on p. 137.

Fig. *101* shows a Monolith or Standing Stone, called Maen Hir in Wales, where there are many of them. Probably they mark graves of important persons but they sometimes represent the sole relic of a Stone Circle or of an Alignment. The latter is a double parallel row of standing stones, a feature sometimes (as on Dartmoor) extending for more than a mile. It is usually found in connection with the circle or the round barrow and points to religious ceremonial. The arrangement of one horizontal stone lying across two uprights, as at Stonehenge, is called a Trilithon.

We have said that Megalithic means building with giant stones, and it is well to realize how large some of these were. Mr. Peet, in *Rough Stone Monuments,* writes of a block weighing nearly 40 tons, which must have been brought 18 miles, at La Perotte, Charente, France.

It may be as well before we pass on to Stonehenge, the greatest of our Megalithic monuments, to

100   A cromlech or dolmen

140

MEGALITH BUILDING

get some idea of how the builders went to work. It is probable that the only mechanical aid they had was the lever. Boys and girls, who learn mechanics, will not need to be reminded of what the lever means, so they must excuse this digression for some others who may not know.

Fig. *102* shows a see-saw, and the principles of leverage may have been discovered by Neolithic, or perhaps Palaeolithic, boys and girls amusing themselves in this way. A see-saw is like a pair of scales; it does not make any difference if you sit on the beam,

101   A standing stone

or are suspended below it. If the two boys sit at an equal distance from the centre, and are of the same weight, they will balance one another, but if one is heavier, he will have to come nearer the centre if equilibrium is to be maintained. So much is this the case, that if he is very much heavier, say 6 stone, to his small brother, 1 stone, then the heavy boy need only be 1 foot from the centre, to balance the light boy at 6 feet (*102*, A). Imagine the beam at A as a lever; 1 cwt. applied in a downward direction at one end, 6 feet away from the centre, will exert an upward pressure of 6 cwt. at the other end, 1 foot away from the centre.

If the boys sit both on one side, as at B, they will be balanced by a 2-stone boy 6 feet away on the other side. If we take the

THE NEW STONE AGE

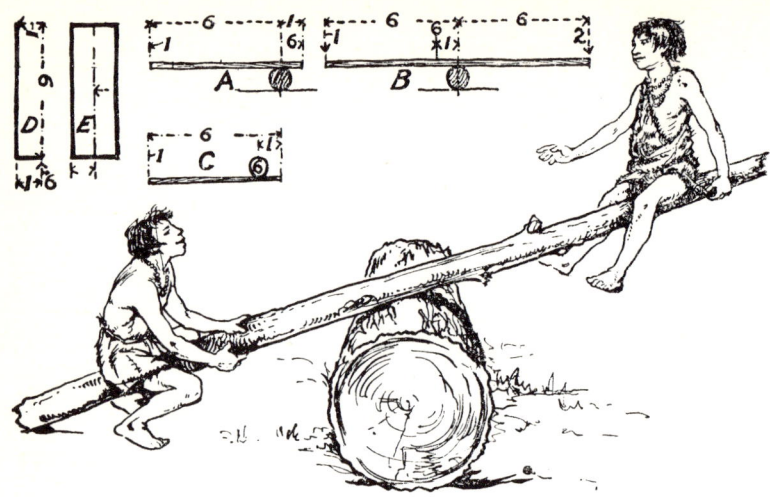

102   The laws of leverage

left-hand side of B, and find that 6 stone at 1 foot=1 stone at 6 feet, and apply it as at C, and imagine the 6 stone at 1 foot as a log or stone which has to be lifted, then 1-stone lift 6 feet away will do it. We can apply our lever in a different way as at D. The beam is bent at right angles; one arm is 6 feet long, and the short one 1 foot. A 1-stone push at the top of the 6 feet long arm will produce a 6-stone pull up at the end of the horizontal arm, 1 foot long. This brings us to the erection of church steeples, chimney shafts, and towers. Take E, 6 units high, by 2 broad in its base, as a tower which has to resist the pressure of wind by its weight. Wind pressures are known, and their force on the whole area is applied to a lever arm of half the height of the tower as at E. To oppose this there is weight, acting through its centre of gravity, on a lever arm of half the width of the base. If the wind pressure is greater than the weight, over goes the tower. We do not say that primitive man looked at problems in this way, but we do, because of the mechanical laws these early builders discovered.

Bearing these laws in mind, we can pass on to a consideration of how the builders went to work. Nature provided a local sandstone, but the inner circle was constructed of strange stones.

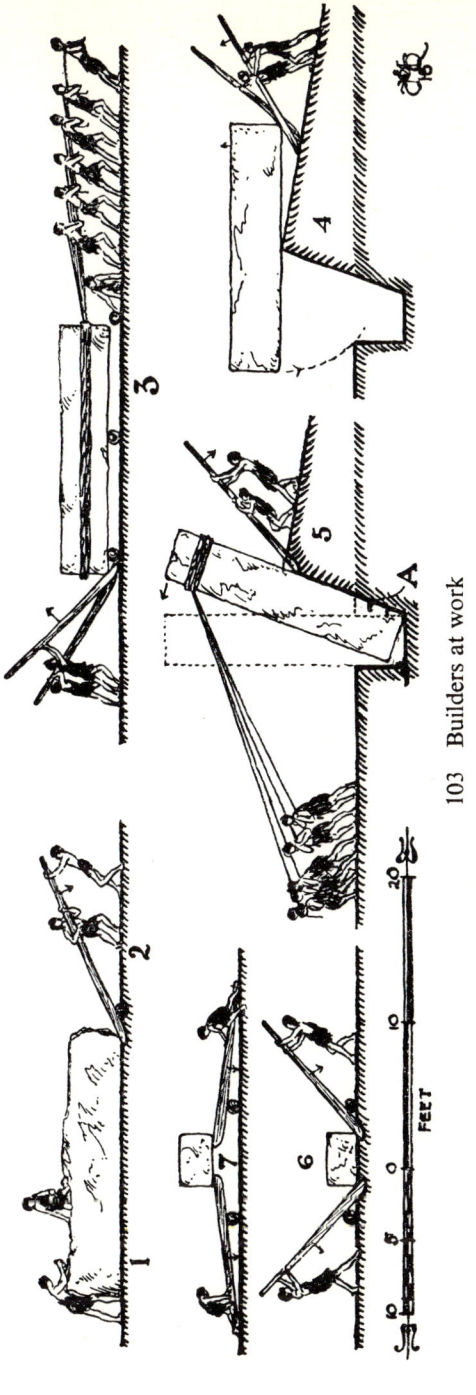

103 Builders at work

THE NEW STONE AGE

The nearest place from which these could have been obtained is the west of Pembrokeshire, and it may be that the stones were already a sacred circle before being moved. Fig. *103*, 1, shows the masons dressing the stone into shape in its original position to save weight in transport. It is thought that the masons used fire first to heat the stone, and then water to make fragments split off, but it would be a dangerous method, and they may have used wooden wedges instead. We have seen a good mason in Inverness-shire working on a large granite boulder on the hillside where it was dropped out of the bottom of a glacier ages ago. The mason wanted to make a 6-inch landing, and he obtained this by drilling a series of holes, into which he inserted wedges, and so split the landing out of the heart of the boulder. The early men perhaps used the same methods, but of this we cannot be sure; we do know that he had flint and stone tools, because these have been found when excavating to raise the fallen stones at Stonehenge. The flint axes were roughly sharpened, and held in the hand, and appear to have been used to clean the surface of the stone, after it had been bruised by larger stone boulders, or mauls, which smashed off the bumps.

Fig. *103*, 2, shows men lifting one end of the block to place rollers under it; 3 shows the rollers in position, and men pulling rough hide ropes, with others behind assisting with levers. At 4 we arrive at the building place, where a hole was dug, having one sloping side, and the upright stone being set in the hole. It was fixed by ramming small stones into the triangular space at A 5, but it seems obvious that a sloping embankment as at 4 must have been built up before the stone could be tipped into the hole. Without the embankment it would be nearly impossible to raise the stone, and a very dangerous job. With the embankment, even if the stone slipped forward a little in the tipping over, it could easily be levered back into the hole, and then when resting against the embankment as at 5, pulling and levering would have raised it; meanwhile earth shovelled down into the triangular space at A would have fixed the stone in the desired position. As to the top lintel stones, these may have been placed in position by making a bigger embankment, or by levers as 6 and 7. The stone raised once could be blocked up, and the operation repeated. The stone shown in fig. *103* is about the size of one of the uprights in the outer circle of Stonehenge. First

STONEHENGE

104 Stonehenge

there is an outer circular ditch and bank, about 300 feet in diameter. There is an opening on the north-east in the circle, where it is joined by an avenue. Within this comes the actual temple. First there is the outer circle, which originally consisted of 30 stones, standing about 14 feet high by 7 feet wide by 3½ feet thick. Around on top of these stones comes the circle of crowning lintels, mortised or hollowed out on their undersides on to tenons or stubs worked on the tops of the vertical stones underneath. Fig. *104* gives some idea of what this outer circle must have looked like when complete. Within this circle is another, of smaller stones, and then came five magnificent trilithons arranged in horseshoe form on plan. Each trilithon consisted of two upright stones and one lintel, and starting from the north-east, or entrance side, the height of the trilithons is increased. Inside the trilithons is another horseshoe of smaller monoliths, around the flat Altar stone.

Just inside the entrance from the avenue is a large flat stone, which has the sombre name of the Slaughter Stone, and a little way down the avenue another upright one called the Hele Stone.

It may well be that Stonehenge was a temple of the Sun, from which the priests or medicine men could take their observation. We accept the longest and shortest days as a matter of course, if we give the matter any thought at all, but not so the Neolithic man. It must have been a mystery to him, that the sun should appear in a shallow arc across the horizon in the winter, but climbs into the sky in summer time. It annoys us on dull days to know that the sun shines behind the clouds and we cannot see it, and Stonehenge may have been a magic observatory, where the priests could determine the position of the sunrise when it could not be seen. The priests may have settled the seasons; have said now is the time to plant; now we will sacrifice to the Sun-god that he may make our crops grow. Again, we accept the miracle of growth and increase as a commonplace, but the Neolithic man, who, in one of his rough hand-made pots, had safeguarded his hardly won seed, did not commit it to mother earth without some offering, or propitiation, or sacrifice. The sacrifice was not necessarily just so much sheer cruelty as an offering to the gods of some person who was loved, or a pot or implement which was valuable, so that the person or family making the sacrifice might be blessed. The individual did not count for very much in those early days; the tribe came first, and if one must die to save the others it had to be. In some such way the sacrifice became a part of the ritual of early religions. We know how in Genesis xxii. 2 God said to Abraham, "Take now thy son, thine only son Isaac, whom thou lovest, and get thee into the land of Moriah; and offer him there for a burnt-offering."

In the twenty-first book of the *Iliad*, Achilles, after he has killed the son of Priam, throws him into the river, and speaking over him "exalting winged words," says, "Nor shall the river avail you anything, fair-flowing with its silver eddies, though long time have you made him sacrifice of many bulls, and thrown down single-hooved horses, still living, into its eddies."

In Mr. and Mrs. Routledge's book on the Kikuyu of Kenya, there is an account of the people who dig for sand for use in making pottery. It is interesting, because it gives us an idea of the spiritual outlook of these people. The natives tunnel into the hillside for sand, like so many rabbits, and as they do not take any precautions, the burrow sooner or later falls in, and smothers the excavator. The Kikuyu do not take any steps to dig the poor fellow out, because this would offend the Spirit of the Sand Pit, but sacrifice a goat instead to propitiate the spirit, then start another burrow which, in its turn, necessitates another goat being sacrificed. This, we think, would have been the case with the Neolithic men: they would worship the Sun, Moon, and Stars, the Rivers and Waters, the Mountains and Valleys, and a great Mother God over all. If by any chance the spirits were

WOODHENGE

offended; if certain things were done which were taboo, or forbidden, sacrifice had to be made.

Stonehenge does not appear to have had any connection with Druidism, which followed many centuries after. The Druids worshipped the Moon and Stars, and Stonehenge was a Sun Temple, built by an agricultural people, to whom the Sun was all-important.

So far as Prehistoric man is concerned, his religion must have

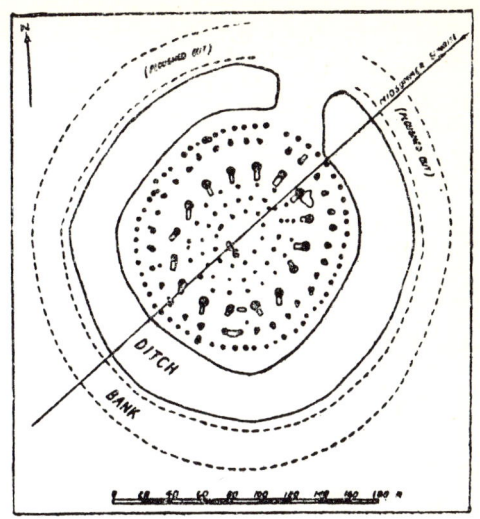

105 Plan of "Woodhenge", Salisbury Plain

been a very real one to him, or he would not have taken so much trouble with the Megalithic monuments we have been describing. These are very widespread, and can be traced along the shores of the Mediterranean, through France, to this country; we have seen how the Picts' towers resemble the Nuraghi of Sardinia (p. 139), and the chambered barrows the Stone Age temples of Malta.

The truth is, of course, that the Megalithic monument form was merely a method of building, and though a great many of the different Megaliths belong to the New Stone Age, others like Stonehenge belong to the Early Bronze Age or, like the Picts' towers, may have been used as a defence against the Romans.

Another type of monument which belongs partly to the New Stone Age and partly to the Early Bronze Age is Woodhenge (*105*). This is in the parish of Durrington, two miles from Stonehenge, and it is the site of a group of wooden circles. There are socketed holes of no less than six concentric oval rings of timber posts, now marked by short concrete pillars. They are surrounded by a broad, shallow ditch and a flattened bank beyond.

THE NEW STONE AGE

The smaller circle at Arminghall, by Norwich, also discovered by Wing-Commander Insull, V.C., has a single horseshoe, once filled by posts twenty or thirty feet high. They both date from the time of the Beaker people.

The plan shows the post-holes (black dots) of the six circles formed by wooden posts at Woodhenge. The "tabs" attached to the larger dots indicate sloping ramps (*103*, A), cut to facilitate the raising of the posts. The G.P.O. cut similar ramps when raising a telephone pole. In the centre of the shrine is a grave in which was found a crouched skeleton facing towards the east with a stone axe-hammer and a beaker (thus establishing a Bronze Age date). Among the finds were two axes made of chalk. These belong to the mystery of the ceremonial. They would have been too soft to use and must have been buried at the outset of the work or the frost would have crumbled them.

This art of building was in its way as wonderful as the La Madeleine paintings described in the earlier part of this book, and we must try and imagine the builders. There is a danger in archaeology of thinking more of the things than of the people who made them; we talk of flint implements, as if the New Stone Age could be collected in a bushel basket and shown in the glass cases of a museum, and especially is this the case in the prehistoric period before there was any written history. The interest of things is that they were made by people, and when the things are temples and tombs they become extraordinarily indicative of the spirit of man; of that essence, or aura, which gives him and his work individuality, and has made possible the great works of architecture, painting, poetry, and sculpture, and which makes it possible for a man to lay down his life for an idea. Any great movement which appeals to the minds of men has always been compounded of the spirit.

Chapter VII

THE BRONZE AGE

WE have seen how the men of the Upper Palaeolithic found a new material in bone and ivory, and the effect of this was to open up a whole range of new activities. They could make harpoons with barbs in bone, which were not possible with intractable flint. Fishermen should place in their calendar of benefactors the Palaeolithic worker in bone who invented the barb.

Even more so the introduction of metal wrought an enormous difference in the lives of men. The edge of the celt might dull with use, but then it could be hammered up again; it did not fly into fragments, and it could be hammered cold, which is an important detail to remember. Trees could be cut down; houses were built more quickly than was possible before, and in a hundred different ways man was given new confidence in his powers and so was able to make progress.

The discovery of metal was as important in its own way as the introduction of steam, or the discovery of electricity.

We must not think of a Bronze Age which started full blown at a particular date, or of a people who threw away their flint implements one day, to arm themselves with metal on the next. It was a very slow and gradual change-over. It is probable that the first flat celts were brought here by traders from the Continent, and many years may have elapsed before they were followed by the round-headed men we now associate with the Bronze Age, and centuries before the first of the Celtic-speaking peoples who reached this country (*see* p. 123).

The art of Bronze working came from the Near East, by way of Italy and Gaul, and was widely spread, except in Africa, which never had a Bronze Age. We have seen, on p. 123, that the Bronze Age men were more powerful physically than the Mediterranean race. Probably they were not all armed with bronze, but in any case in the end they conquered the Neolithic people. It was not a conquest of extermination, because we find in the round barrows, which are typical of the

THE BRONZE AGE

Bronze Age, round-headed men side by side with long-headed Mediterranean men.

A parallel can be found in Greece, where the Achaeans of the Heroic Age dispossessed the Minoans of Mediterranean stock.

As the art of metal working is the great central fact which has given the name of the Bronze Age to this period, it may be as well to start with a description of the methods followed by prehistoric man in his craft; in doing so we must try and place ourselves in his position, and imagine that we have never seen metal before. Bronze, we know, is an alloy of copper and tin, and we shall find that copper, like gold, is sometimes found almost pure, and is capable of being hammered up cold, without any preliminary smelting to reduce the ores. Iron ore is found in the form of red earth, or stone, and is not so obviously metallic, and would more easily have escaped attention than copper. The North American Indians hammered up pure copper, and made knives in this way before the coming of the European invaders. So the age of bronze may have been preceded by one of copper. Even when smelting and casting bronze had been discovered, it was found that it could be forged cold, and that when it was heated, it tended to become brittle and fly to pieces when being hammered. It is hardened by hammering, and softened by heating and quenching, whereas iron hardens by heating and quenching. Bronze was an ideal metal for prehistoric man, because dulled edges could be hammered up again anywhere without very much trouble. It can be made extremely hard.

We can now pass to smelting. Pottery had given man the idea of taking a plastic material and shaping it; he may have used clay to line a cooking-pit, and found that baking hardened it. In the same way the accidental introduction of copper ore into a cooking-pit, or a charcoal fire exposed to the wind, would have melted the ore, and this would have been found as metal when the ashes were raked aside. The metal may have cast itself into a shape which suggested a tool or weapon, and it would have prompted the ingenious man to experiment. In some such way it must have come about. The first moulds were simple flat open moulds, into which the molten metal could be poured, then progression was made to hollow casting with clay cores

BRONZE SMELTING

which could afterwards be scraped out. Stone, bronze, and probably fine sand were used, and actual moulds can be seen at the British Museum.

We get an inkling of how the Bronze Age men went to work from the *Iliad*, xviii. Hephaistos, the famed artificer, who "wrought much cunning work of bronze, brooches and spiral arm-bands, and cups and necklaces", when he starts work on the wonderful shield for Achilles—"went unto his bellows and turned them upon the fire and bade them work. And the bellows, twenty in all, blew on the crucibles, sending deft blasts on every side.... And he threw bronze that weareth not into the fire, and tin and precious gold and silver."

This would have been an apparatus very similar to that used for iron at the Glastonbury lake village(*146*). Copper melts at 1083° centigrade, and tin at only 232°, so that the Bronze Age founder melted the copper first, then threw charcoal on to the melted mass to retain the heat, and added the tin. The ideal aimed at seems to have been 10 per cent tin to 90 per cent copper, but endless experiments went to the discovery that this made a good bronze. Prehistoric man did not know anything about analytical metallurgy. Surface copper ores sometimes contain tin-oxide, and the intelligent man would soon have been moved to find out why an axe made from this ore was tougher than one of pure copper.

We can now discuss the actual implements made, and fig. *106* shows

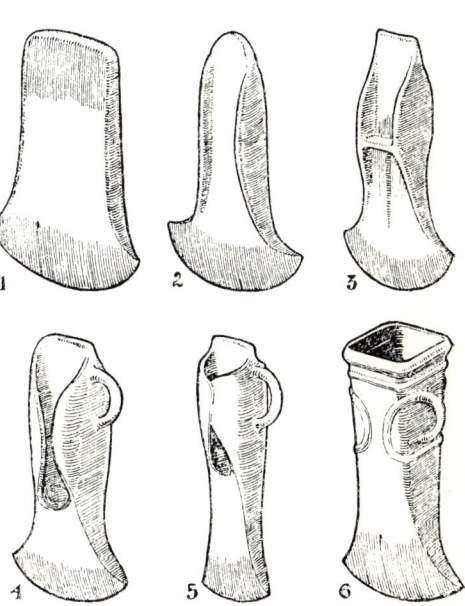

106   Development of Bronze axe

THE BRONZE AGE

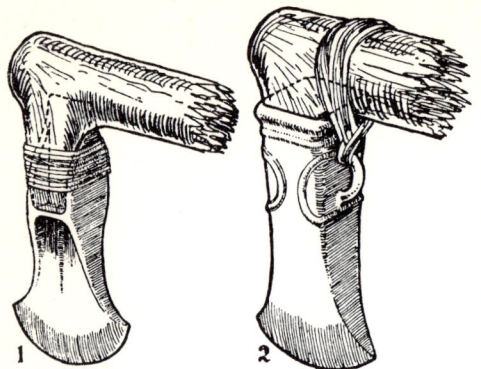

107 Hafting of palstave and socketed axe

the development of the Bronze Axe No. 1 is called the Flat Celt, and is obviously fashioned on the lines of the stone axe which preceded it, and was hafted in the same way as fig. *107*. The makers soon discovered that by hammering the edge it became thinner, keener, and wider, so the upper part of the later celts is narrower.

No. 2 shows the Flanged Axe, formed by hammering over the sides. This was hafted as fig. *107*, 1. A stick with a stout branch was selected, and this being cut off, was forked to fit over the top of the axe, and bound to it by raw hide. The disadvantage was that the thin axe split the wood head. A stop ridge was then developed between the flanges, and this finally developed into fig. *106*, 3, which is known as a palstave, from an Icelandic word for a narrow spud. This stop ridge took the force of the blow, and prevented the head from splitting(*107*, 1). In this type, the web between the flanges, above the stop ridge, was thinner than the axe part under, and this feature is more pronounced in 4, where the flanges are hammered over into the form of what is known as the Winged Axe. No. 5 shows the wings lapping, and in 6 they have disappeared, and we arrive at the final Socketed Axe, which was hafted as fig. *107*, 2. There were endless intermediates, and the axe is well worth studying, because it is the ancestor of the tool which is still in use today.

The Bronze Spear is a weapon with an interesting history. It started life as fig. *108*, 1, and in this form was used either as a knife or a dagger. It was cast solid, and provided with a tang which was fitted into the end of the wooden shaft, and this latter was prevented from splitting by a plain bronze collar, through which a rivet passed and secured the end of the tang. In 2 the collar has become socket-shaped, and though not cast with the spear-head, is attached to it by two rivets, and the tang still

THE BRONZE SPEAR

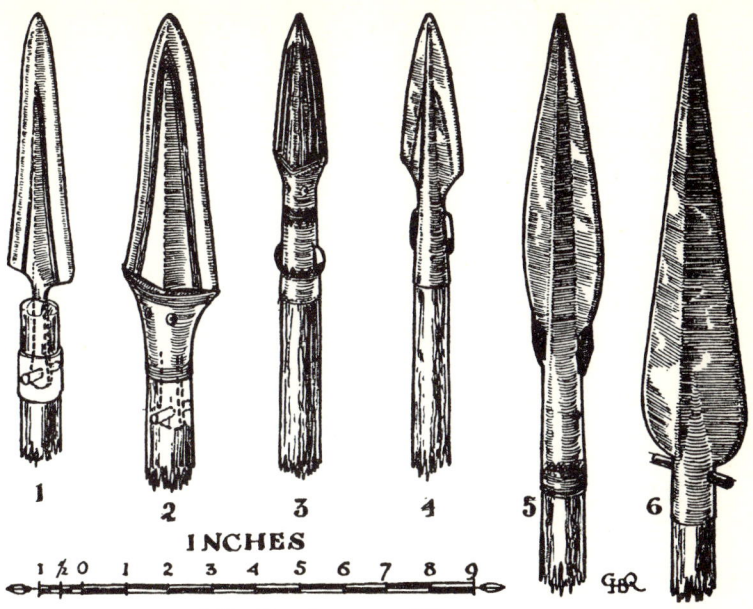

108   Development of Bronze spear

remains. In 3 the tang has gone, and the socket is part and parcel of the spear-head. But an amusing fact should be noticed: that the rivets which once fastened it to the head remain as ornamental bumps; 3 has loops for thong attachment to the shaft, or for tying on feathers or streamers. In 4 and 5 the socket has further developed, and the spear-head is formed of fins cast on to the sides of the socket. In 5 these are leaf-shaped, and the loops are decorative. In 6 the whole spear-head is a triumph of hollow casting.

The sword developed out of the knife by way of the dagger or rapier. It is easy to see that spear-head No. 1 (*108*), if it had a short handle fitted on to the tang instead of the shaft, would make a useful knife. A rapier was an elongated dagger, and the sword a later invention. Fig. *109* shows a beautiful leaf-shaped

109   A leaf-shaped sword

THE BRONZE AGE

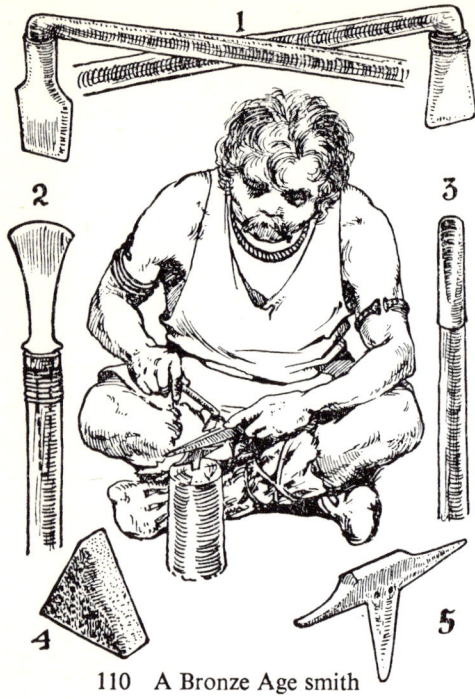

110   A Bronze Age smith

sword. The tang for the handle was cast on the blade, with the edges slightly flanged up, and then in between these edges grips of horn or wood were riveted on each side through the tang, and a round pommel clipped on to the end. Leather scabbards were used with bronze tips called chapes. Bronze was not used for arrow-heads, but flint, as in Neolithic times. The two drawings, fig. *106* of the axes, and fig. *108* of the spears, show the development over the whole of the Bronze Age, and this lasted not less than 1300 years. To realize how long a time this is, we must remember that 1300 years ago in this country would take us back nearly to the time of the death of Ethelbert, king of the Kentish men, and the first English king who received baptism.

These swords and spears are the beginning of the history of Arms and Armour. In the Stone Age men were probably, like the Eskimo, so engaged in finding enough to eat that little time was left for quarrelling about their scanty possessions. With the introduction of metals they could make more things, and life became easier and they had more time for fighting. These Bronze Age arms must have been used in the way described in the *Iliad*.

A flanged axe with slight stop ridge, a type midway between 2 and 3, fig. *106*, was found with a spear-head slightly earlier in form than fig. *108*, 3. The archaeologist in this way, by associated

HEATHERY BURN CAVE

finds, builds up a theory of the dates and developments of civilizations. Fig. *110*, drawn from the actual tools at the British Museum, shows the equipment of a Bronze Age metal-worker. At 1 are his hammers, hafted like socketed axes. 2 shows a tanged chisel, and 3 a socketed gouge; 4 is a sandstone rubber, and 5 an anvil.

One of the most interesting discoveries ever made in England was what appears to be the complete furnishing of a family at the end of the Bronze Age. This was found in Heathery Burn Cave, County Durham, which may have been used as a house, or as a place of refuge. From remains of skulls which were discovered, the inhabitants appear to have been long-headed men of Mediterranean or Neolithic stock, and it is possible that they removed to the cave in face of the danger of invasion. We shall see later how, at Glastonbury, a people of similar extraction were put to the sword by invaders.

The Heathery Burn discovery included a sword much the same as fig. *109*, but with slight shoulders on the cutting edge of the blade near the handle; a leaf-shaped spear-head, as fig. *108*, 5, but without the loops; bronze discs 55 inches diameter, which may have been used as dress ornaments or horse trappings; bronze collars which fitted on to the nave or hub of chariot wheels, and which, in conjunction with the bridle bit, show that the horse was used. A bucket was found, and tanged and socketed knives; a razor, a gouge, and a socketed axe as fig. *106*, 6, chisels, awls, pins, rings, tongs, and gold armlets. There were bone prickers, spindle whorls, skewers, knives, the cheek-bars of bridle-bits, and jet armlets; and all these things can be seen at the British Museum. This splendid find includes nearly all the known types of Bronze Age implements, and we have founded our illustrations on these Heathery Burn discoveries.

The spindle whorl shows that spinning was practised in the Bronze Age in this country; both spinning and weaving are supposed to have started in the Swiss lake dwellings as early as the Neolithic times. Various types of dress fastenings began to come into use which were suitable for light woven fabrics. Fig. *111* shows a bronze brooch from Ireland, shaped rather like a large hollow curtain-ring, and so arranged that a bronze pin could be passed through it, and in this way fasten a cloak drawn

THE BRONZE AGE

through the ring. This type may have suggested the penannular brooch (*149*).

In a barrow of this period in the East Riding of Yorkshire, the remains of a linen winding-sheet were found under a skeleton, and woollen fabrics have been found in others; these could only have been woven on a loom. We will consider, then, the steps which a Bronze Age weaver had to take if she wished to convert a fleece into a piece of stuff for making clothes. It would need washing and cleansing first, and then came dyeing. Crotal, a lichen growing on trees, may have been used. If this is put in a pot with the fleece and water, and boiled for one or two hours, it produces a rich red-brown colour. Teasing consists of pulling the fleece into fluff, and oiling explains itself. Carding is an operation which consists of putting the wool on an implement rather like a large butter-pat with teeth, called the card, and then pulling the other card across it, so as to arrange the wool for spinning. This latter was the occupation of girls for so many centuries, that we still talk of an unmarried woman as a spinster.

The spindle which was used in the Bronze Age consisted of a piece of wood, perhaps about 1 foot long and $\frac{1}{2}$ inch diameter, and a few inches from one end came the whorl, which acted as a miniature fly-wheel and helped to twist the spindle. At the other end was a little nick in which the yarn was fastened. In spinning, a

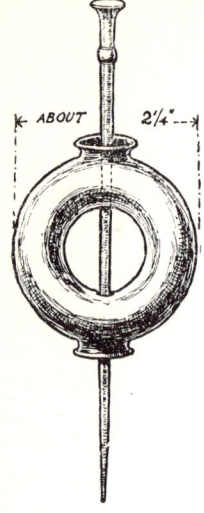

111 Bronze brooch and pin

112 Spinning

WOVEN CLOTH

roll of carded wool was held in the left hand, or bound on to a distaff; from this roll a little wool was pulled out and twisted by the fingers until a piece of yarn was made about 18 inches long, and this was tied to the spindle. The wool was then paid out with the left hand, and the spindle twisted with the right. When the spindle stopped revolving it was held, when the twist ran up the length of wool which had been paid out and made this into yarn, which could then be wound on to the spindle and the spinning resumed (*112*).

Weaving is, and has been since the Bronze Age, one of the crafts which has had the greatest influence on the progress of man. It is beautiful work, done wherever man wants clothes, and carried out in many different ways; but the main principle of weaving is always the same. The long threads running through the length of a piece of cloth are called the warp; the ones which cross these by going under and over the warp are called the weft. From the discovery of loom weights, as shown at the bottom of the warp-threads in fig. *113*, in the Swiss lake villages and in England, it is thought that the earliest looms were of this pattern, which is called the Warp-weighted Loom—the weights keeping the warp properly stretched. The warp-threads were kept in place by yarn threaded through them at the bottom. It is probable that at first the weaver took the skein of yarn in her right hand, and picking up the warp-threads one or two at a time with the left hand, passed the weft-threads through from side to side, over and under the warp. She may have used a wooden lath to beat the weft-threads up, and so make the cloth compact.

113 Warp-weighted loom of simplest type

THE BRONZE AGE

114 Warp-weighted loom of more developed type

Fig. *114* shows the next development, and our drawing is based on the Scandinavian loom in the Copenhagen Museum. The diagrams at the side, A and B, illustrate the method of weaving, and we shall find as we go along that, though the details are elaborated, this principle remains. A piece of fabric has been woven from the top downwards, and below this the warp-strings hang down with their weights on the ends. They are divided at 1 by a shed-stick: the shed is the space through which the weft is passed. At 2 is the heddle-rod, which is attached to alternate warp-strings by loops. The weaver then passes his shuttle through the space between the warp-strings, above the heddle-rod in A position, which is called the counter shed. The heddle-rod is then pulled out to B position, which brings the warp-threads which were at the back to the front, and the weft is again passed through the space now called the shed.

In this way the weaving proceeds, like darning, first under and over the warp-strings, then over and under. This would make a plain cloth; in patterned work different coloured yarns can be used, and instead of just over and under the warp, you can go over and under and then skip two or three, and so produce a pattern. On Greek vases Penelope is shown working at an upright warp-weighted loom like fig. *114*, but it has been

WEAVING COMBS

developed by making the top cloth beam to revolve, so that the cloth could be wound up as it is woven.

Fig. *115* shows what is called now a weaver's comb, found at Glastonbury lake village, but we doubt if this was used, as suggested, to comb or pack the weft-threads tightly together; it would have been an inconvenient way of doing it; so here is a problem for our readers to determine the use of the comb.

Fig. *116* is taken from a Bronze Age drawing on the side of a bronze vessel. This is very hard to understand since it is drawn in straight lines, but if you look very carefully you will see three triangular women engaged in spinning and in weaving with just the same sort of loom as we have drawn for you. The remains of dresses of this period have been found in Jutland, which suggest that the piece of stuff woven on the looms was wrapped around the body without any shaping. This is the case with the tunic of the man and the skirt of the girl. In the case of the man this was the beginning of the kilt. The girl's bodice would have been roughly cut in kimono shape, and the side seams sewn under the arms. She might wear a bronze disc fastened on to a woven tasselled belt, with her hair gathered into a thread net,

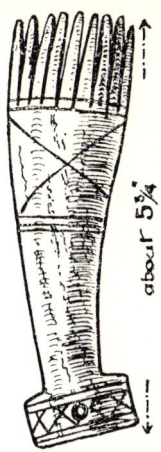

115   A comb

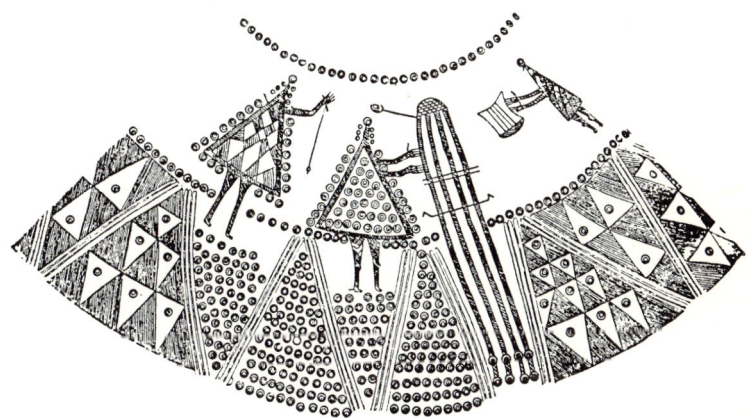

116   A Bronze Age drawing of women weaving

THE BRONZE AGE

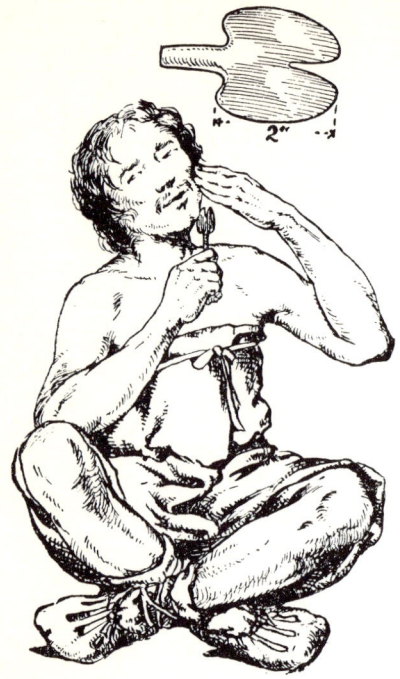

117 Shaving with Bronze razor

and fastened by long bronze pins. The shoes of both man and woman were of skin, and the man had a circular cloak and cap of thick rough knotted wool.

Fig. *117* shows a man shaving with a razor of a very usual pattern in England during the Bronze Age; he probably used oil instead of soap.

We have seen on p. 155 that one of the finds at the Heathery Burn Cave was a point of deer antler, about five inches long and curved in shape; it is pierced twice on the radial lines of the curve, and once at right angles. Similar pieces have been found in the Swiss lake dwellings, and it is suggested that these were the cheek-bars of bridle-bits. Probably the first bit was a twisted leather thong, knotted at the width of the mouth, and then the ends passed through the cheek-pieces as reins. If the transverse hole of one of these horn bars is examined, it will be found to be worn smooth as by a leather rein. Similar cheek-pieces are described in the *Iliad*.

The Heathery Burn discovery includes bronze nave collars for chariot wheels. The nave of a wheel is its hub, and this suggests spokes. The first wheels were probably solid on their axle, rather like a cotton reel. Fig. *118*, A, shows another type made up of three boards secured by dovetailed clamps. Fig. *118*, B, shows the start of the spoke, not as we know it today, but arranged more as a brace. The upright part includes nave, two spokes, and parts of the felly or rim, all in one piece of wood. The four other spokes are braced between this and the remaining parts of the felly. These came from the Swiss lake dwellings, and must be early types, because a later wheel has been found there

CHARIOT WHEELS

which, though in bronze, must have been founded on a wooden construction. It is 19¾ inches in diameter, and has four spokes radiating between nave and fellies, just like the wheel of today. We know too that beautifully turned wooden wheel naves have been found at Glastonbury lake village, dating from the Early Iron Age, and in what are called the chariot burials of Yorkshire, of the same period, the iron tyres of chariot wheels have been discovered.

The original Aryan-speaking peoples, the forerunners of the Celts, are supposed to have possessed ox-wagons, and it may well be that chariots were introduced into England during the Late Bronze Age between 700 and 500 B.C.

It is interesting to see the drawings Bronze Age men did of these chariots. We illustrate two of these drawings (*119, 120*). The first, scratched on a broken piece of pottery, shows a chariot used in a funeral. The dead man has been burnt and put in a large container on the chariot. The chariot is drawn by two horses and the dead man's charger is being led in front of the chariot, just like the Duke of Wellington's charger that carried him at Waterloo was led at his funeral a hundred years ago. The second drawing is a rock carving showing two-wheel war chariots, and a four-wheel cart drawn from above. The artist did not know how to draw the wheels properly in this position, so they are placed sideways so that you can recognize them.

The chariot does not give very much opportunity to the maker to vary its shape. There must be a floor framed up on the axle, around which would come the body, perhaps of wickerwork covered with hides. There would have been a centre pole, with yoke attachment to the horses. The chariot of classical times must have been founded on some such simple basis.

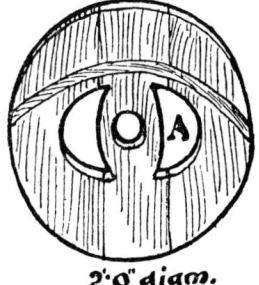

2′·0″ diam.

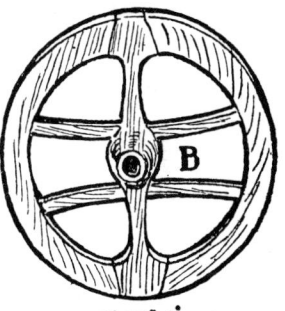

2′·10″ diam.

118 Wooden wheels

THE BRONZE AGE

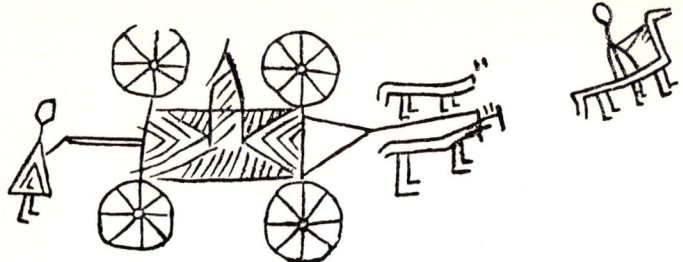

119   A funeral procession engraved on a piece of broken pottery

Again we cannot do better than turn to the *Iliad* for an idea of how chariots were used.

This question of wheel naves, the discovery of jet armlets at Heathery Burn Cave, and shale cups in round barrows, all of which must have been turned, brings up the question of lathes, It is difficult to see how a simpler turning contrivance than the pole lathe(*151*) could be made, and this may date from the Bronze Age.

We know little of the tracks these chariots must have used, though Bronze Age Corduroy-roads of planks have been found preserved in the marsh peats of East Anglia, and fords may have been replaced by bridges; there are two on Dartmoor which are still called Celtic. Fig. *121* shows one of these at Postbridge, and its construction is just what we should expect from a people who had inherited the building tradition of Stonehenge. We should like to draw attention to the trumpet

120   A rock engraving of two chariots and a four-wheel cart

121 A clapper bridge

THE BRONZE AGE

shown in the hands of one of the figures. These instruments derive their shape from the horns of animals, which had been used for the same purpose before. They were made at the end of the Bronze Age, in that metal, and are supposed to have been used by the Celtic people in warfare; of two types, some have the mouthpiece at the side.

The possession of the bronze axe, with its better cutting powers, meant that man could make ever larger clearings in the forest, grow more corn, and keep more herds. He was helped again, because with his bronze sickle the harvesting of his crops was not such a problem as when that useful implement was of flint (*90*). There is a beautiful harvest scene in the eighteenth book of the *Iliad*—"where hinds were reaping with sharp sickles in their hands. Some armfuls along the swathe were falling in rows to the earth, while others the sheaf-binders were binding in twisted bands of straw. Three sheaf-binders stood over them, while behind boys gathering corn and bearing it in their arms gave it constantly to the binders; and among them the king in silence was standing at the swathe with his staff, rejoicing in his heart. And henchmen apart beneath an oak were making ready a feast, and preparing a great ox they had sacrificed; while the women were strewing much white barley to be a supper for the hinds." Game was less eaten now than the domesticated animals; a proof that life was becoming easier, and

122   A plough

PLOUGHING WITH OXEN

it was not necessary to live by the chase. There are Scandinavian and Ligurian rock carvings of Bronze Age date, which show a primitive plough drawn by oxen. One of these which we have copied for you, shows an aerial view or plan of a man ploughing with two oxen (*123*). You can see the plough in his hand, and another man in front shouting to the oxen to hurry them up. Archaeologists believe that the introduction of the plough is the greatest change that took place in prehistoric times after the discovery of farming. The plough came into Britain in late Bronze Age times just before the introduction of iron. At the same time the first real fields are discovered—the little *Celtic Fields* still seen on the Salisbury Plain (*137*)—and the population in England increased about ten times in this period. This is because the introduction of the plough made farming more efficient—much more corn could be gathered from the fields, and so more and more people could live in Britain.

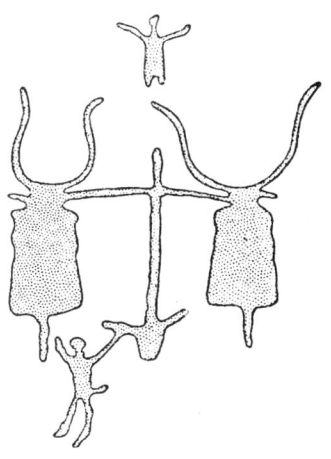

123 Rock engraving of a man ploughing with oxen, as seen from above

Pottery was still hand-made, without a wheel, but ornament was improving, and consisted of straight lines arranged as chevrons, lozenges, herring-bones, with dots and concentric circles (*124*). Fig. *125*, 1, is of a beaker, or drinking-vessel, which was introduced on the East Coast by the Beaker people (*see* p. 120); it is found with unburnt burials; 2 is a food vessel; 3 a cinerary urn, made to hold the ashes of a cremated burial; and 4 an incense cup. This does not mean that the Bronze Age people used incense, and the name has been suggested by the pierced treatment of the little cups; these are found in round barrows, and may have been used to bring the sacred fire which started the funeral pyre. It is thought that these types of pottery, which were doubtless deposited with the dead, for their use in the spirit world, are similar to those they used in their everyday life. Bronze implements were buried for the same

THE BRONZE AGE

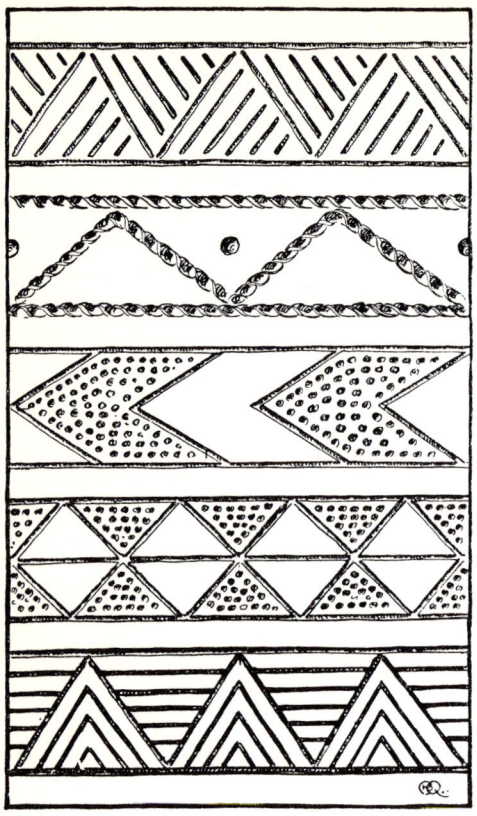

124   Bronze Age pottery ornament

reason, but were generally limited to plain axes, knife, daggers, and awls, and this limitation points to some symbolical meaning in those selected.

Burial was either by burying the body (inhumation), or by burning it (cremation), and it is a little bewildering to find both methods practised at the same time, because inhumation is distinctly Neolithic, and cremation a Celtic custom, and yet this latter was practised before the Celts arrived. This points to a survival of the long-headed people and their ways, and the introduction of cremation as a fashion by the earlier round-heads from the Continent. A pit was dug in the ground, and a stone cist was made of four stones on edge covered by another, or a hole cut in the chalk, and the ground heaped over in the form of a round barrow. In a stone country, the barrow was made of heaped stones, and became a cairn. Fig. *126*, 1 is the type which is called a Bowl Barrow, because it is like an inverted bowl; 2 a Bell Barrow, because the ditch and bank made around the outside give it that shape; and 3 is a Disc Barrow.

A barrow is sometimes called a Tumulus; in Derbyshire, a Low; and in Yorkshire, a Howe.

ROUND BARROW POTTERY

Silbury Hill, 6 miles west of Marlborough, on the Bath Road, is in the form of a round barrow, but it is 135 feet high, and covers 6 acres. It is wholly artificial, and in 1907, at the rates of pay then obtaining, its cost was estimated at £20,000.

Cup and ring markings are common on the cover stones of the cists or graves in the barrows, and these are very similar to the markings found on the *churingas* of the Australian aborigines (p. 69).

Small objects called Sun Discs are found in Ireland; these are made of gold about $2\frac{3}{4}$ inches diameter, and have the same decorative idea as the cup and ring markings, made up of concentric circles. All these things point to Sun-worship being characteristic of the Bronze Age; another symbol, which is widely distributed, is the swastika, also considered a symbol of the Sun.

It must be borne in mind that prehistoric man was still held in thrall by magic and mystery; that there were many things which were taboo or forbidden; like the Kikuyu his life and death were governed by a complicated ritual. Cremation in all probability was not practised to destroy the body, but to purify

125   Bronze Age pottery

THE BRONZE AGE

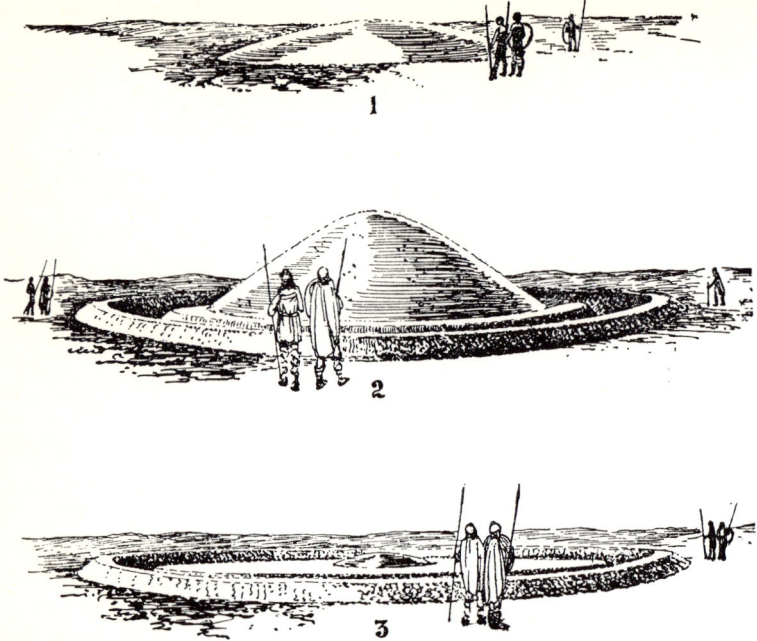

126 Bronze Age barrows

it of sins and uncleanness, and render the spirit fit for the life hereafter. In the twenty-third book of the *Iliad* the spirit of the hapless Patroklos appears to Achilles and urges him: "Thou sleepest and hast forgotten me, Achilles. While I lived never did'st thou forget me, and only now that I am dead. Bury me with all despatch, so that I may pass the gate of Hades. Far do the spirits keep me off, the spirits of men out-worn; they suffer not that I should join their company beyond the River; and vain are my wanderings through the wide-gated house of Hades. Pitifully I beg that thou should'st give me thy hand; never again shall I come back from Hades, once you have granted me my due of fire." We have seen that the implements which were buried with Bronze Age man were limited to certain symbolical types. Again we find that in the actual cinerary urns were buried, with the human remains, the bones of wild animals, like the fox, mole, and mouse; surely these typified something. In the barrow itself, the bones of the ox, goat, sheep, horse, pig, and dog have

THE BURIAL OF HECTOR

been found with cremated burials; of these some may be the remains of the funeral feasts, and the horse and dog may have been slaughtered to accompany their master, and the sacrifice of slaves and captives may have formed part of the ceremony. Bone pins have been found, charred by fire, as if they had fastened the body in its shroud before it was burned.

Homer, in the twenty-fourth book of the *Iliad*, gives a wonderful picture of the burial of Hector:

"So nine days they gathered great store of wood. But when the tenth morn rose with light for men, then bare they forth brave Hector, weeping tears, and on a lofty pyre they laid the dead man, and thereon cast fire.

"But when the young dawn shone forth, rosy-fingered Morning, then gathered the people round glorious Hector's pyre. Assembling, they first of all quenched the flames of the pyre with wine, even as far as the might of the flames had reached, and thereupon his brethren and friends gathered his white bones, mourning him with big tears coursing down their cheeks. The bones they took and laid away in a golden urn, wrapping them up in soft purple robes, and quickly set the urn in a hollow grave, and heaped above great stones, closely placed. Then hastily they piled a barrow, while everywhere about watchers were posted, through fear that the well-greaved Achaians might make an onslaught before the time. And, when the barrow was piled, they went back and, assembling, duly feasted and well in the palace of Priam, that king fostered by Zeus. Thus did they hold funeral for Hector, tamer of horses."

In the twenty-third Book even fuller details are given of the funeral of Patroklos, and the funeral games—of how they went forth "to hew high-foliaged oaks with the long-edged bronze", and "splitting them asunder the Achaians bound them behind mules", and so brought the wood to the appointed place, and made a great pile. "And they heaped all the corpse with their hair that they cut off and threw thereon." The pyre was "a hundred feet this way and that, and on the pyre's top set the corpse." "And many lusty sheep and shambling crook-horned oxen they flayed and made ready before the pyre; and taking from all of them the fat, great-hearted Achilles wrapped the corpse therein from head to foot, and heaped the flayed bodies round. And he set therein two-handled jars of honey and oil.

THE BRONZE AGE

leaning them against the bier; and four strong-necked horses he threw swiftly on the pyre, and groaned aloud. Nine house-dogs had the dead chief: of them did Achilles slay twain and threw them on the pyre. And twelve valiant sons of great-hearted Trojans he slew with the sword" to be consumed by the fire. The North Wind and the loud West "all night drave they the flame of the pyre together, blowing shrill", and after a barrow was made as already described for the burial of Hector. Then followed the funeral games, of which all can read in the twenty-third book of the *Iliad*. The next time we see a round barrow, we must think of it, not as only so much heaped earth, but rather as a visible sign of our own Heroic Age. We must try and conjure up a picture of the flaming pyre, and looking across the smoking eddies of time, see the crowd of Bronze Age warriors burying their chief.

Figs. *127, 128* and *129* show the remarkable and extensive early Bronze Age tumulus of Bryn Celli Dhu, another variety of burial monument in use at this time. There was a large outer

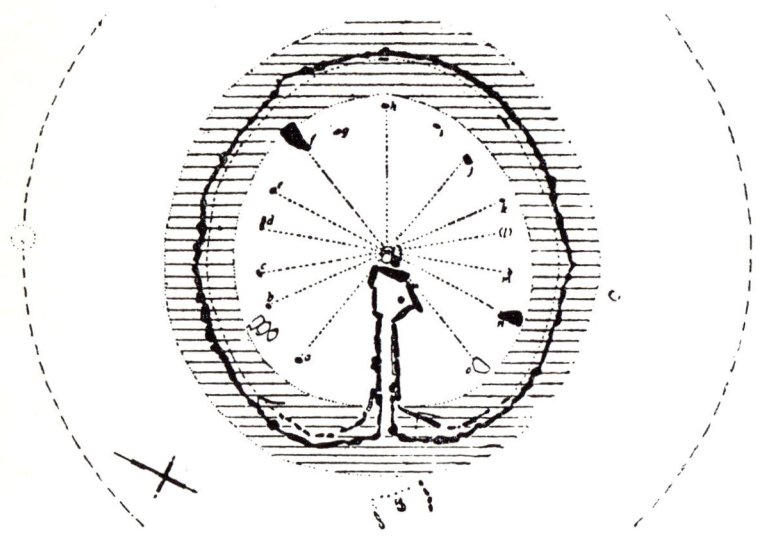

127 Plan of the chambered cairn of Bryn Celli Dhu, Anglesey

BRYN CELLI DHU

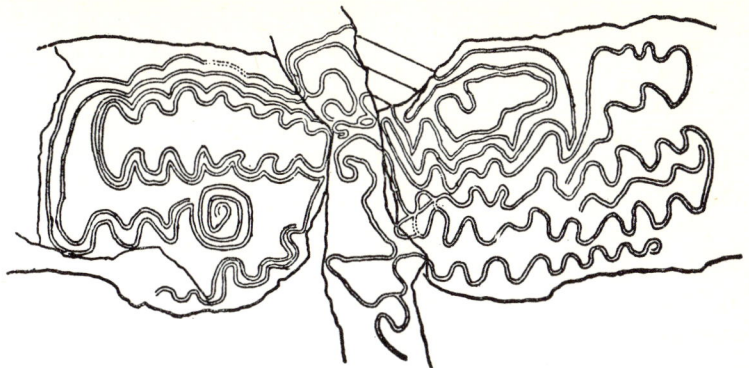

128 Diagram of markings on the pattern stone, Bryn Celli Dhu

circle of standing stones (now gone). This was in full view. The three other circles were hidden in the mound covering the burial chamber. The two next circles indicated by heavy black and light broken lines (*127*) consist of upright stones with dry stone walling between them. Actually they are not circles for, when traced out from end to end (including the passage and chamber in the heart of the mound) they are found to form a continuous spiral—a magic cypher! The innermost circle is of single stones. At the foot of some of them the burned bones of young persons were found. The dotted lines connecting them show how they are arranged in opposite pairs in line with the centre of the whole tomb. To one side of the inner chamber will be noticed a recess to make room for the black dot. That dot is a tooled pillar standing five foot six inches above ground (*129*). The stone with the design illustrated in fig. *128* is shown just beyond the chamber and by it another at the very centre of the whole tomb. This covered a small pit containing two large lumps of red jasper.

129 Pillar stone in chamber of Bryn Celli Dhu

THE BRONZE AGE

Just outside the entrance to the passage was the skeleton of an ox, its head turned towards the portal. The Ministry of Works has restored the chamber and the covering-mound. The date is about 1500 B.C., and the monument seems to represent the amalgamation of many cults of the circle and the barrow.

We will now try to give our readers some idea of the migrations and minglings, the traffic and trade routes, which had developed in the Bronze Age from the earlier Neolithic beginnings. We must first ask ourselves why it is we find these big movements of men, because, leaving on one side the adventurous few, the general run of people do not move until they are pushed. In the Old Stone Age, man moved because he was a hunter, and had to follow the chase to live, and in the same way, even when he had settled down, he could not be sure of a permanent home, unless it was accompanied by a perennial food supply; if this failed, then he had to break fresh ground. If food were one of the reasons for his moving, he naturally went away from the crowded central area, or falling on his neighbours compelled them to do so. Wars have played a terrible part in migrations; we have seen in our time great movements of people, as a result of the 1939–45 struggle. The study of these movements is of great value as bearing on the original homes of men. That is why the archaeologists continually do dig; they are hunting for first causes.

Geography will help us to discover the natural causes of man's movements on certain lines. On p. 32 we referred to the Loess land. Loess is a sandy, chalky loam, deposited at first as dust blown by great blizzards from the glaciers in the Ice Ages. This loess is in a broad zone, which, starting from the Ural Mountains, stretches across South Russia to the Carpathians, and the Danube, then through north-west Austria to south Germany, and the north of France. The fine grain of the loess prevented the spread of forests, and became instead the great grasslands which have played so considerable a part in the development of Europe. Here have been bred great hordes of men, who in times of drought, or when the regions became overpopulated, have descended on the ancient civilization of the East, and caused movements of men. In the same way, the Arabian Desert has been a great reservoir of hardy people, who

130 Female Clothing

131 Male Clothing

BRONZE AGE CLOTHING

132 Bronze Age Toy Boat

133 Bowl made into a model of a Bronze Age Ship, with Circular Shields hanging over the side

134 Underside of Ship Bowl with Sea-waves, Oars above and Ship's eyes

BRONZE AGE GEOGRAPHY

periodically have made exodus, with terrible happenings to their prosperous neighbours, or have been bribed to keep the peace.

The problem which confronts such a people is similar to that of the hill-tribes of the North-West frontier of India. Here the Mohmands, Afridis, Wazirs, and Mahsuds, perched on the barren hills, can only live by levying tribute on the caravans passing from the fat lands. Here through the great land gate of the Khyber Pass, through all the ages, immigrants have gone into India. The Aryans, and Alexander: all travelled on this line until a new way was forced by sea.

If along a certain line similar kinds of pottery or stone monuments are found, it is fair to assume that these are the work of a particular type of people moving along this line. If in Bronze Age barrows we find gold from Ireland, glass or beads from the Mediterranean, amber from Scandinavia, or in an Early Iron Age cemetery at Aylesford in Kent, a bronze flagon from north Italy, it points to trade and trade routes. We may be sure that salt was traded.

We have already written, on p. 120, of one of the earliest migrations, that of the Mediterranean people; also of the first of the round-heads, and of the arrival of the Beaker people; and, on p. 121, of the movements of the Ayran-speaking peoples. This brings up another factor of great importance in the lives of men, and one which is not concerned so much with their movements, as with the circulation of some great idea that acted as a lever, and caused them to alter their mode of living. The wonderful drawings and paintings of the Aurignac and La Madeleine Periods in the Old Stone Age, which we discussed earlier, and the Megalithic buildings of the New Stone Age, were wrought around some central inspiration; again, in the latter half of the Bronze Age, the prophets were at work, and we find the introduction, by the Aryan-speaking peoples, of cremation and all that it may have implied. The Minoan civilization was centred in the island of Crete, the home of Minos, and then transferred to Mycenae on the mainland of Greece. The Cretans were of the Mediterranean stock; their power declined about the 1500th century B.C. Their buildings were Megalithic, and they did not cremate their dead. While the Minoan civilization was dying, we hear of the beginnings of the Heroic Period of the Hellenes. Jason, Agamemnon, Hector, and

THE BRONZE AGE

Odysseus are typical of wild men who came from the north, finding their way down from the grasslands, and they were an Aryan-speaking people who cremated their dead. The Achaeans were followed by the Dorians, who destroyed the Mycenaen civilization in Greece, and settling down became the Spartans. There were great movements of the Celts, Gaels, or Gauls, in the Early Iron Age. They were a Nordic people living to the north of the Alps, and called by the Romans for this reason Transalpine. They sacked Rome in 395 B.C., and were typical of the barbarians across the Danube and Rhine who were to become a constant menace to the Empire later on.

If the Mediterranean men found their way through Gaul, a later route seems to have been from Marseilles (Massilia) by the Rhône Valley to Châlons, where it divided into three lines; one to the west down the Loire, the second around the Paris basin, and the third through the Belfort Gap, between the Vosges and Jura Mountains, and down the Rhine. This latter route is an important one, because it mingled people coming up from the Mediterranean with another type coming from the regions to the north of the European and Asiatic Mountains.

Professor Fleure thinks that the Beaker people came from Kiev on the Dnieper, south of the Pinsk Marshes. Their settlements have been found on the tributaries of the March in Moravia; on the Bohemian tributaries of the Elbe by Prague; around the junction of the Saale and Elbe; the mouth of the Oder; on the Zuyder Zee; and again at the junction of the Rhine and Main. In the British Isles pottery beakers of the same type are found on our eastern coasts from Caithness to Kent, and also found on the west coast of Scotland.

The west coast of Denmark, and the south Baltic, supplied amber during the Bronze Age, and the two main trade routes pass through Germany to the Adriatic. One started from Venice, up the valley of the Adige, through the Brenner Pass, down the Inn to Passau on the Danube, and then by way of the Moldau to the Elbe, and so to Denmark. The second route was from Trieste to Laibach and Graz, then to Pressburg on the Danube, from there up the River March, across Moravia and through Silesia, along the Oder, then across Posen to the Vistula, and Danzig. The spiral design of the Bronze Age found in Scotland, Cumberland, Lancashire, Northumberland, south Ireland, and

LAND AND SEA VOYAGES

Merionethshire, and which was common in Egyptian and Ægean art, is supposed to have found its way here on the first of these two routes.

We can now pass from land journeys to sea voyages, and we will work back from Caesar's time. It was the Veneti, maritime tribesmen occupying what is now Vannes, Morbihan, in Brittany, who formed a confederation of the tribes in north and north-west Gaul against the Romans. The Veneti seem to have controlled the trade with Britain, and possessed a fleet of large ships with leathern sails, high poops, and towers, but did not use oars, which was the reason they were beaten on a calm day by the Romans.

If we go back again to the time of Pytheas of Marseilles, about 330 B.C., we find that he sailed to Britain, and there was in his time a regular trade between Cornwall and Marseilles, and probably a sea-borne trade between Cornwall and Cadiz (Gades) which was a centre of the tin trade. From Cape Finisterre, Pytheas sailed east along the north of Spain to Corbilo on the mouth of the Loire, past Ushant to Land's End (Belerium), where he landed. He sailed all round Britain, and attempted an estimate of its circumference, and indicated the position of Ireland. Long before this, as we have just seen, the Beaker people came across the North Sea, and settled on our East Coast; so even the prehistoric period had its great seamen and sea-faring traditions. We illustrate (*132-4*) two boat models from this period. The first is a little wooden model of a river canoe, with the Bronze Age warriors standing up in it, holding their shields and spears. The second is a wooden "boat" with a beaten gold cover, on which you can see the shields of the warriors hanging over the side of the ship, the oars or paddles, and even the waves of the sea. At the prow of the ship are two large eyes serving to bring good luck to the vessel on her journey.

This discussion of the trade routes enables us to take up the question of the position of the Cassiterides (from the Greek word for tin, *cassiteros*), or the tin islands of the ancients: were they really islands? The Greeks and Romans obtained tin from Galicia, Cornwall, and possibly the Scillies, but the main supply was from Cornwall, and possibly it is the British Isles which were the Cassiterides.

THE BRONZE AGE

Pytheas says tin was conveyed by the people of Belerium in wagons, at low tide from the mainland, to the island of Ictis, where it was purchased by merchants, carried to Gaul, and transported on pack-horses to Marseilles, the overland journey taking thirty days. To start with there has been considerable doubt as to the locality of Ictis; some think it was St. Michael's Mount, others the Isle of Wight or Thanet. The tin must have been mined in Cornwall, and it would have meant a long overland journey to the two latter places.

We have seen there were good sailors, and the general weight of evidence inclines us to accept the view that the tin was shipped at St. Michael's Mount, close to where it was mined. The fact that the Veneti formed the confederation against Caesar points to a predominance based on trade, and they may have controlled the tin traffic, in which case Corbilo would have been a natural place for unshipment.

From Corbilo to Marseilles is approximately 500 miles, which means nearly seventeen miles a day for the pack-horses on the thirty days' journey. The tin was cast into ingots, of the shape of ankle bones, and two of these made up the load for a pack-horse.

Britain has always been rich in metals. Copper is found in Cornwall, Cardiganshire, Anglesey, Snowdonia, and in Ireland. Tin in Cornwall and on Dartmoor. Prehistoric man would have obtained his copper from boulders, or found lumps of ore on the hillside, and tin from the gravel beds of streams. Ireland was El Dorado of the Old World, and gold was found in the Wicklow Hills as late as 1795. It was shipped across to Carnarvonshire, or the mouth of the Mersey, and from there found its way down by way of Shrewsbury, Craven Arms, Wootton Bassett, Sarum, and a deeper and more navigable Avon to Christchurch, and so across to Cherbourg. Another route appears to have been from the Mersey, across the Peak District to Peterborough and the Wash, where it was shipped to Denmark and north Germany.

It is interesting to see how, by mapping the finds of bronze implements, and gold ornaments, trade routes are established. Sea-borne traffic is shown by the large number of hoards of bronze implements, found near the sea coast, and around the estuaries of navigable rivers.

TRADE AND TRADE ROUTES

Going right back to Neolithic days, we find that flints were mined at Grime's Graves (Grime means the devil) in Brandon and at Cissbury near Worthing, and apparently only roughly chipped there and then exported to be finished elsewhere. They must have been carried along the trackways to the hill forts. These old trackways have interesting names. The Ridgeway comes from Fenland along the Dunstable Downs to Berkshire, the White Horse, and the Marlborough Downs; there is the Harroway coming from Cornwall, and finding its way through Hampshire to the Thames estuary; and the Pilgrims' Way, along the southern slopes of the North Downs, was an old road long before men tramped its surface to Becket's shrine at Canterbury.

Here we must attempt to sum up what we have found out about the Bronze Age. The introduction of metal opened up new activities for man, and especially new opportunities for the individual. The Neolithic man toiled with antler pick and shoulder-blade shovel, and piled earth in the banked camps. He chipped sarsen stones, and fidgeted them into the upright position of menhirs and dolmens. It was patient team work in which everyone laboured for the community. He needs must move from camp to camp to find pasture for his flocks. In much the same way primitive peoples like the Tasmanians, Australian aborigines, and the Eskimo are fully occupied in hunting to live; they have not any leisure for fighting, or any possessions to fight for. When everything has to be carried about, the lighter you travel the better.

The earlier round-heads appear to have been powerful, and may have been a pleasant people; we have seen that they were buried side by side in the same barrows with the older stock of Neolithic long-heads, and this points to friendly conditions.

As metal became more plentiful, larger clearings were made in the forests, and man began to settle down. He could grow more crops and keep more cattle; he began to have possessions. This was the opportunity for the individual; if a man was harder working than his fellows or more far-seeing, cleverer or more frugal, he could become a man of property, and, founding a family, become the chieftain. The tribe was gradually forged into a nation, and the chieftain became a petty king. With these added riches and possessions and the temptations they brought, we find the first traces of really warlike weapons, and it is probable that the Bronze Age saw the beginning of organized warfare.

We may be sure that this wider life brought in its train a set of problems which had not confronted the Neolithic herdsmen. As man began to have more possessions, he becamed alarmed for the safety of his own, or envious of those of others.

These people give proof of being able to work together, and so may have attempted, in a gradual way, to solve the problem of the right mode of living. Without some code or tradition, the community would have degenerated into a rabble. We shall find as we go along that man is tremendously concerned with this, and seeks many ways for his own government. We shall not be far wrong if we picture the Bronze Age people as living, like the Homeric Greeks, under kings and nobles, yet given some share in the framing of the law.

Chapter VIII

THE EARLY IRON AGE

HERE we must start by another reminder: that at the beginning of the Early Iron Age, which first saw the introduction of that metal, men did not pack up all their old bronze implements and bury them in hoards, to at once arm themselves with iron. It was, on the contrary, a very gradual change-over, and for a long time both bronze and iron were used side by side. This was so at Hallstatt in the Noric Alps of the Austrian Tyrol. Here there have been salt mines from the earliest times, and it must have been an important trading centre. Excavations have been carried out in the cemetery of the salt miners, and the implements found there have been held to be distinctive of the civilization at the beginning of the Early Iron Age, when bronze was still in use.

The second half of the Early Iron Age is held to be most typically shown by implements which have been recovered from an old settlement, built on piles, on the margin of a bay on Lake Neuchâtel, near Marin, to which the name of La Tène, or the Shallows, has been given. The finest developments of the Early Iron Age are to be found in this country, since it fell under Rome's influence at a later date than the Continent; in the same way the Iron Age, or Late Celtic tradition, survived in Ireland and parts of Scotland which were never occupied by the Romans.

The people of England had become very mixed racially. On p. 120 we sketched the order of the arrivals of the different peoples; and just as bronze overlapped the use of iron, so the old peoples carried on their everyday life and were not always exterminated by the new-comers or even dispossessed of their lands. We saw how, in the early round barrows, the later round-heads were buried side by side with the earlier longheads.

The next arrivals were the Goidels, or first of the Celtic-speaking peoples. On p. 124 we mentioned the generally accepted theory that they were driven into the west by their

THE EARLY IRON AGE

successors, the Brythons, who were related to them and spoke another variety of the Celtic language. This is now being given up, and it is thought that there were never any Goidels in England or Wales, but that they went directly to Ireland, the Isle of Man, and Scotland, where their Celtic descendants still live.

The Brythons were followed by the Marnian Celts who were responsible for the finest developments of what we now call Late Celtic art, and by the Belgae who were the latest of Britain's pre-Roman invaders. They came from where Belgium now is, and had more Nordic blood than their predecessors; they were a half-Teutonic and fierce fighting people.

We saw on p. 155 how the people of the Heathery Burn Cave were of long-headed stock, which yet had absorbed a Bronze civilization. Much the same thing occurs in the Iron Age at Glastonbury lake village, and we shall base our illustrations of the period on the houses and implements discovered there.

In Neolithic times the idea of building over water was developed, and in Switzerland there were dwellings built on the margins of lakes. They were first discovered at Ober-Meilen, Lake Zürich, in 1853, and this started research, and the discovery of similar structures in different parts of Europe. These may be divided into three types. (1) The Swiss dwellings, built on platforms formed on the tops of piles driven into the lake bed or more often into the marshy land at the edge of the lake, which date from the Neolithic and Bronze Ages. (2) Another type in which, instead of pile foundations, large open framings resembling log huts were sunk in the lake and steadied by piles, much like the modern caisson used by engineers for foundations. Dwellings of this type were built in France and Germany during the Early Iron Age. (3) The type like Glastonbury and the Scottish and Irish Crannogs. These were really small islands formed in the middle of marshes and, being stockaded around, were raised above the flood-level by earth brought from outside; but the foundation was quaking bog, which, as we shall see at Glastonbury, gave the inhabitants a great deal of trouble. These date from the Early Iron Age, and continued to be occupied in remote spots, as places of refuge, until the seventeenth century.

135 Iron Age Man

136 Celtic Shield from Battersea

137 Aerial view of Celtic Fields

138 Aerial view of the Celtic Hill figure at Uffington

LAKE VILLAGES

As the Swiss lakes became overpopulated, people moved downhill into the Po Valley, and here are found the settlements which are called Terremare, from *terra marna*, or marl earth. The peasants discovered that the earth from these old settlements was valuable for agricultural purposes, and in carting it away came across antiquities which disclosed the secret.

There are literary references to lake dwellings. Caesar said, writing of the Morini (a Belgic tribe in Gaul, opposite Kent): "They had no place to which they might retreat, on account of the drying up of their marshes (which they had availed themselves of as a place of refuge the preceding year), and almost all fell into the power of Labienus" (*Com.* iv, c. 38).

Venice itself, the Queen of the Adriatic, is a glorified crannog which started as a place of refuge. "They little thought, who first drove the stakes into the sand, and strewed the ocean reeds for their rest, that their children were to be the princes of that ocean, and their palaces its pride."

Hereward the Wake maintained himself, in the last stand against the Normans, in the marshy recesses of the Isle of Ely.

Now we come to the interesting way by which we in England came to be provided with a lake village of our own. Mr. Arthur Bulleid of Glastonbury, when he was a young man, read Keller's *Swiss Lake Dwellings*, and was fired with the idea that there must have been a lake village in the olden days in the swamps near Glastonbury. Remember that in this neighbourhood there is the tradition of Arthur and his knights and the Isle of Avalon:

> "The island valley of Avilion,
> Where falls not hail or rain, or any snow,
> Nor ever wind blows loudly."

So whenever Mr. Bulleid went on his walks abroad he kept a wide-open eye for any indications of a possible site for a lake village. This was in the end discovered by the mounds which had been left where the hut foundations were, and though in the course of 2000 years or more the land had been drained, and became covered with vegetable soil and turf, yet these mounds were still noticeable to the observant eye. In the molehills were found pieces of bone and charcoal, and when Mr. Bulleid made

139 Glastonbury lake village

THE DISCOVERY OF GLASTONBURY

a trial hole he came across more charcoal, some pottery, and two oak beams. Again, a labouring man, David Cox by name, told Mr. Bulleid that when he had been cleaning out a ditch about three-quarters of a mile away, in 1884, he had found a black oak beam embedded in the soil, and had to cut a piece off it to widen the ditch. Cox reported that this beam looked like the end of a boat, and this is what is turned out to be(*143*). So Mr. Bulleid's dream had come true, and he had found his lake village. Excavations were started in 1892, since when the village has been thoroughly explored.

Fig. *139* gives a bird's-eye view of the village. The area was about 10,530 square yards, and the foundations of the enclosed space were reinforced with layers of logs, laid down crossways, and filled in with brushwood, stones, and clay, but it could never have been what the land agents describe as a "desirable building site". During the time that Glastonbury was occupied, a bed of peat accumulated in some places 5 feet thick, and the inhabitants were constantly rebuilding. The village was palisaded around, with piles driven into the peat, and filled in with wattle and daub. This method was also used in the construction of the huts—there were 80 to 90 of these, roughly circular in shape, and varying from 18 feet to 28 feet in diameter; they may not all have been houses; some were probably used as barns or workshops. The huts contained a central hearth (*140*) of flat stones let into a clay bed, and as many as nine or ten hearths have been found added one on the top of the other, as the foundations settled down into the bog. The wattled walls of the huts were daubed with clay; this is known because pieces of clay showing the marks of the wattles were discovered in the excavations. Each hut had a central pole or roof tree. We can gather little more than this.

We have to look to a primitive people, then, to find parallel building traditions. The Kikuyu, of Kenya, today build and live in houses which must be the same as those at Glastonbury. Fig. *141* shows these on the left-hand side of the section, and on the right is the suggested form of the Glastonbury hut. We have made this drawing from the plan and carefully detailed particulars in Mr. and Mrs. Routledge's book, *With a Prehistoric People*. It is an interesting fact that the constructional problem which the Kikuyu have to face, when they build their huts, is

140 Hut interior at Glastonbury

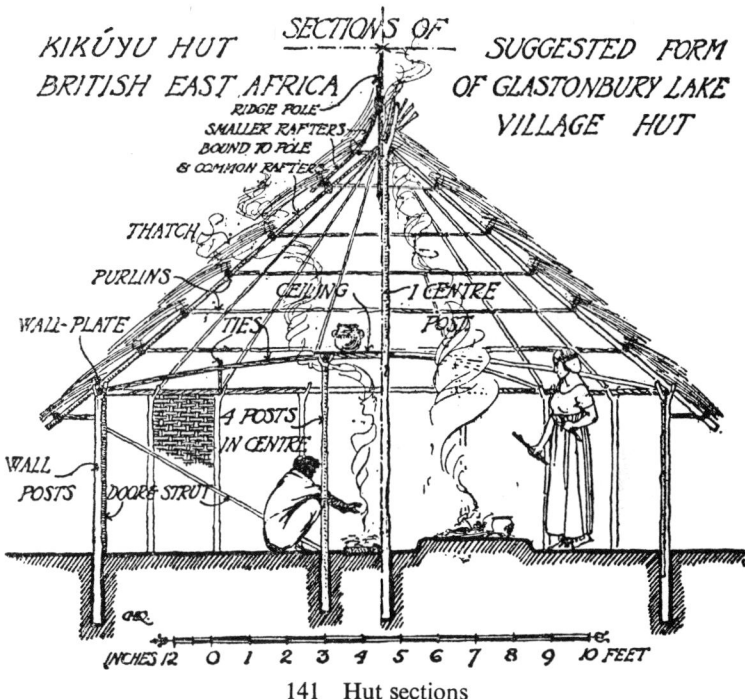

141 Hut sections

similar to the one which confronted Wren when he designed the dome of St. Paul's Cathedral.

Neolithic man sometimes built little houses with rafters leaning against a central pole, and this was a very sound method. So long as the feet of the rafters were firmly fixed into the soil, the house stood firm, in gales and under a load of snow; the drawback was that there was no headroom around the walls, and so one had to sit there as in a bell-tent. A wall was raised around to give headroom, and this was satisfactory so long as the wall was built of stones heavy enough to provide a sufficient abutment for the thrust of the rafters. The trouble came when the same idea was attempted with thin wooden walls, which would have been overturned.

The Kikuyu first set up about nineteen forked posts in holes dug in a circle of about 15 feet diameter. To appreciate the cleverness of the construction, you must remember that none of the wood is thicker than a man's arm. Four posts are set up on an

THE EARLY IRON AGE

oblong in the centre about 4 feet 5 inches by 3 feet. Around the tops of the outer posts, long pliant rods are woven, and these form the wall plate, and take the thrust of the roof. Again ties are woven from this wall plate across from side to side, picking up the tops of the centre posts on the way. Wren took up the thrust of the brick cone which supports the dome and lantern at St. Paul's, by an iron ship's cable, which was let into the stone, and run in with molten lead. The rest of the construction of the Kikuyu hut is explained by the drawing.

At Glastonbury there were also found remains of an earlier type of hut, built with wall plates resting on the tops of piles driven into the peat. The huts were apparently oblong in shape, with hurdled walls mortised to the wall plates. Of these we cannot attempt any reconstruction, but of the circular huts we can be more sure, and it seems fair to assume, from what we know, that they resembled those of the Kikuyu.

This building in wattle and daub continued as a tradition throughout Celtic Britain. William of Malmesbury, writing in

142   Building a hut at Glastonbury

143 Dug-out canoe and landing-stage at Glastonbury

THE EARLY IRON AGE

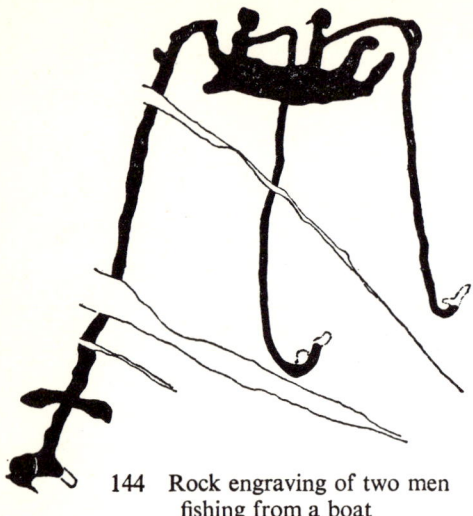

144 Rock engraving of two men fishing from a boat

the twelfth century A.D., mentions the "Ealde Chirche", the ancient church of St. Mary of Glastonbury, built in the seventh century, of wattle-work.

We know that the Glastonbury people used canoes, for one was found by David Cox, to which reference has been made, and some form of canoe would have been absolutely necessary to the inhabitants of the village. Judged by the peat deposit, all this district around the River Brue must have been a vast morass in the olden days, and in times of flood an inland sea. The canoe(*143*) is of the greatest interest—about 18 feet long, the flat bottom is 2 feet wide, 10 feet from the prow, and its maximum depth inside is 12 inches. It is becoming boat-like, and shows a notable development on fig. *75*, having a shapeable prow, and a graceful rise, or sheer, at bow and stern. The lake villagers had a landing-stage and dock attached to their home, with vertical walls made of stout grooved oak planks driven into the peat, into which were fitted horizontal boards(*143*). We know they went fishing, because lead net sinkers have been found. Their canoes would have been used to take them to their cornfields on the mainland; the island village had no room for these. A rock engraving drawn at the time shows two people fishing from a boat. You can see their fishing lines, and the boat has an anchor with a cross-piece and a heavy stone weight on the end, like some in use today. Many querns and millstones have been found; the earlier type(*91*), and the later rotary types(*145*). In these the lower stone was fixed, and had a wooden pivot in the centre. The top stone was fitted over this, and corn fed through the hole, made large enough to allow it, passed down, and was

VILLAGE LIFE

ground between the upper and lower millstones, coming out at the sides as flour. Small cakes were found at Glastonbury, made of unground wheat grains which had been mixed probably with honey and baked.

The villagers also owned horses; many harness fittings have been found, bits, and the wheels of chariots. Whether the horses were transported to the mainland on rafts or stabled there we cannot be sure. In the summer they may have been pastured on the mainland, within the protection of a camp, and in the winter ferried across to the village to share the huts with the inhabitants. The people doubtless used their canoes to carry on trade with the surplus goods which they manufactured and wished to exchange for other commodities. The two iron currency bars found point to this (*see* p. 216).

145   Grinding corn

When we pass to the life carried on within the village, we have proof of many and varied activities, but it will perhaps be well to start by a description of the iron working, which gives the period its name.

Fireclay crucibles have been found at Glastonbury, and funnels (*tuyère*) for conducting the blast into the furnace, but it is thought that the crucibles were used for melting copper and tin, to make bronze, as described on p. 151.

So far as iron working was concerned, it is probable that this was carried out as the present-day smelting operations of the Kikuyu of Kenya, which we have shown in fig. *146*. The iron ore is collected from surface workings in the form of an iron sand; this is washed to get rid of the clay and other substances, so that the iron grains are left. The furnace consists of a kidney-shaped hole in the ground lined with clay. The ore is placed in the pit

THE EARLY IRON AGE

146 Smelting iron

of the furnace, and a charcoal fire started, then more ore and charcoal are added as needed. The blast is introduced at one end of the furnace, which is slightly lower than the middle, by means of a fireclay funnel (*tuyère*). In the funnel are introduced the wooden pipes of the bellows, which are in this way protected from the fire. Two bellows are used, of goats' skins sewn into the shapes of rough cones, or fools' caps, the pipes being attached to the small ends. At the larger ends of the bellows, which are open, are fitted two short sticks, sewn to the skins, but leaving one-third of the circumference free. The smiths' boy holding the two sticks of the two bellows, two in each hand, opens first one bellow, as if the sticks were hinged at one end, and then the other, and closing the opening by shutting his hand, depresses the sticks, and kneads the ends of the bellows, sending forward a continuous blast into the furnace. This blast raises the temperature of the furnace, just as a fire is brightened up by ordinary bellows.

The ore is reduced to a sticky mass rather than molten metal; furnaces which will generate a sufficient heat to make the metal flow only date from the seventeenth century, and we do not find any cast iron before then. The lump of iron is left in the furnace overnight to cool, and then turned out in the morning, and broken up into sizeable pieces which are forged up into ingots or blooms. This iron is very pure, and ductile, and so can be readily forged; being smelted with charcoal it is free from the

METAL WORKING

sulphur which comes from coal when it is used, and which makes the iron short and brittle. The fireclay crucibles we have referred to were buried in a hole in the ground, and the fire and blast arranged as in the case of the iron smelting.

In Messrs. Bulleid and Gray's book are shown illustrations of all the finds in the excavations, and here we can see daggers, spear-heads, swords, knives, bill-hooks, sickles, saws, gouges, adzes, files, bolts, nails, rivets, keys, and bits. The weapons are few and far between, and this is perhaps one of the reasons the villagers fell an easy prey to their enemies in the end. The man in fig. *140* is holding an iron bill-hook in his hand, of a quite modern shape; and fig. *147* shows one man using a curiously shaped saw, with the teeth arranged so that it cuts on the upstroke, while the other has an adze, which is first cousin to the axe. Fig. *148* shows a man using a particularly beautiful iron knife found at Glastonbury.

Leaving iron working, we can turn to bronze, which still continued in use in the Early Iron Age as it does today.

Fig. *149* shows a penannular (almost a ring) brooch. The top drawing shows how the pin, which was loose on the ring, was pushed through the material, and then fastened by moving the ring round a little, and clipping it under the pin. This form of brooch was the forerunner of the buckle.

Fig. *150* shows three bronze brooches, or *fibulae*. These

147 Saw and adze

THE EARLY IRON AGE

148 An iron knife

fastenings came into use in the Swiss and Italian lake villages when cloth was first woven. The three examples drawn here show the development of these pretty little things, which the archaeologists associate with the lake village of La Tène, on the lake of Neuchâtel, and are called types 1, 2, and 3, though only type 2 occurs at La Tène itself. In 1 the foot is bent back until it touches the bow of the brooch. In 2 the end is no longer free but actually attached to the bow, and in 3 the foot and bow are designed as one.

On the right-hand side of fig. *150* we have drawn the development of the springs of these brooches, and in each case the pin of the brooch is shown vertically. In those of Hallstatt the springs are on one side of the head; those of La Tène are bilateral: 1 shows the earliest type, like that of a safety-pin of today; 2 has a double coil; and in 3 the pin has one coil to the right, and the wire is then carried to the left, where, after a treble coil, it swings up to form the bow of the brooch. In 4 there is a double coil on both sides, and in 5 a treble coil, but the tension is increased by the ingenious way in which the loop or chord across is taken under the arch of the bow; the whole pin—coils, loop, and bow of the brooch—being in one unbroken length. In 6 we have pin and coils to the right, the loop or chord and the coils on the left in one piece; but the bow is a separate part which is hooked under the chord: 8 is on the same principle, but the spring is covered with a metal sheath attached to the bow. In 7 the bow is fixed

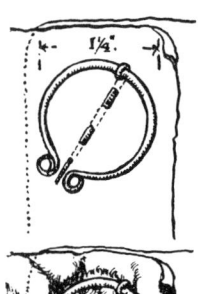

149 Penannular brooch

DEVELOPMENT OF THE BROOCH

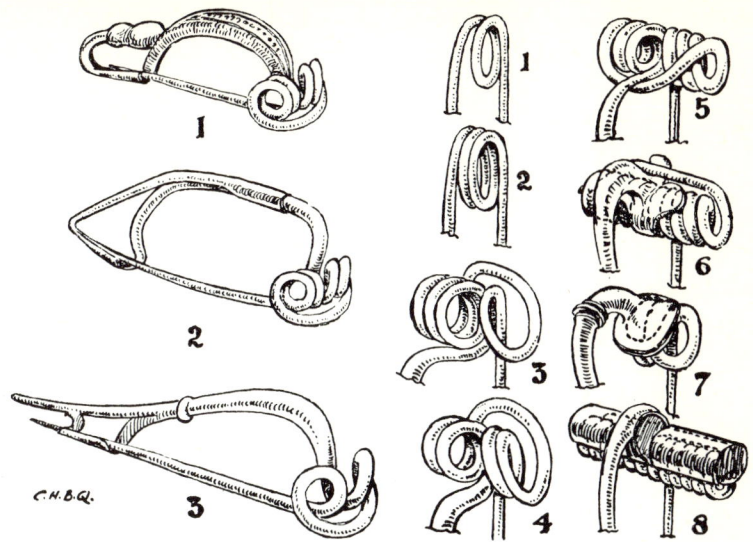

150 Brooches and brooch springs

on to a smaller loop. We consider these springs of the greatest importance: 1 dates from perhaps as early as 400 B.C., and 8 takes us up to the Roman occupation, and, so far as we know, 1 is the first application of the spring. The old brooch-maker who, in 400 B.C., tapped his bronze wire around a rod and discovered the spring, would have been rather surprised if he could have looked into the future and seen the many ways to which his invention would be applied; for example, that we should tell the time by little spring-driven machines, which we call watches.

There were excellent potters at Glastonbury, and fig. *140* shows some of the pottery found there. The greater part of it appears to have been hand-made, as described on p. 124, but the very beautiful pot in the foreground has been turned on some sort of wheel. We saw (p. 124) how the Kikuyu build up their pots on a pad of leaves, which makes it possible to turn the pot round as it is being made, and it is probable that the potter's wheel was preceded by a turn-table, on the lines of the rotary quern (*145*). If a heavy block of stone or wood were

THE EARLY IRON AGE

pivoted in this way, its weight would aid the momentum of its spin and be very helpful in making pottery. This early type is suggested in fig. *161*, A.

Spinning and weaving were carried on in the village, and the spindle whorls and loom weights suggest that this work was done as already described on pp. 156–8.

There were expert coopers at Glastonbury, who knew how to build up tubs with wooden staves and hoops. They were good turners. There is a turned bowl, shown in the lower right-hand corner of fig. *140*, which was decorated in addition with a beautiful running pattern cut in an incised line. There is no evidence of what the Glastonbury lathe was like, but fig. *151* shows a very primitive type in use in the Chilterns, called the pole lathe. It is difficult to see how anything could be simpler than this, and it is obviously a development from the bow-drill(*41*). In the Chilterns the men who make chair legs buy a fall of beech in the woods, and to save cartage build themselves little huts and turn the chair legs there. The supports for the lathe are often two trees growing close together, which they cut down at a height suitable for the two planks forming the bed of the lathe, into which the poppet heads are fixed. A third sapling is bent down, and the cord, which is to transmit the power, is fastened to this, passed around the chair leg, and connected to the treadle under. A rough tool-rest is provided. The turning is done on the down stroke, which revolves the chair leg towards the turner, and when he takes the pressure off the treadle, the pole pulls it up again ready for another cut. The work proceeds very rapidly, and we have seen chair legs turned as fast as one a minute.

In our sketch we have shown the turner making a wooden bowl, like the ones which were used before the days of enamelled iron. The block of wood was placed directly against one centre of the lathe, and on the other side came a circular piece of wood, around which the cord was passed; this was put on to the other centre of the lathe and fixed to the block for the bowl by four brads. This, we think, shows that the so-called Kimmeridge coal-money is the core left from turning shale bracelets on pole lathes. Coal-money is found near the Kimmeridge shale beds

151 A pole lathe

THE EARLY IRON AGE

on the Dorset coast, and consists of circular discs, having a hole on one side, and a square recess or two or three smaller holes on the other. The diagram at the bottom of fig. *151* shows how we think a shale bracelet was turned on a pole lathe. AA are the poppet heads, and BB the centres, C is the circular piece of wood around which the cord was passed, fitted on to one centre, and let into one side of the piece of shale, in a square recess, or by two or three separate pins, the shale being in contact with the other centre. The turner trued up his bracelet, and set its outside shape first, and then making a cut on each face, finally detached it as dotted line D, and the Kimmeridge coal-money was the useless core, and never used as money. One great advantage of these old pole lathes was that the turner could make two or three bowls in graduating sizes from the same block of wood.

The Glastonbury carpenters used axes, and we do not realize in these days what a useful tool this can be—that is, to a craftsman and not a wood butcher. Alex. Beazeley, an architect, wrote in 1882 that the Swedish carpenters at Dalcarlia and Norrland, "require no other tools than the axe and the auger, and despise the saw and plane as contemptible innovations, fit only for those unskilful in the handling of the nobler instruments: they will trim and square a log forty feet long as true as if it had been cut in the sawmill, and will dress it to a face that cannot be distinguished from planed work." We shall find the truth of this—so long as man is master of his tools we get good work, but when the machine masters the man we have indifferent results.

The form of lake villages suggests that they were built by timorous people, living in fear of fiercer neighbours. They appear to have had their beginnings with the long-headed Mediterranean race of the New Stone Age. The Glastonbury lake villagers belonged to the Marnian Celtic stock who inhabited much of Britain at this time, and were famous for that highly decorated and enamelled woodwork. The Marnian Celts are believed to have come from the valley of the Marne river, north of Paris. We illustrate(*135*) a man of similar racial stock found in another bog like those around Glastonbury but actually in Denmark. The peat has preserved the body perfectly,

THE FALL OF GLASTONBURY

as it preserved the Glastonbury houses—we can tell from the contents of his stomach what he had eaten, and his face provides us with the first prehistoric portrait from the life. These men were small and dark—5 feet 3 inches to 5 feet 8 inches in height—oval-headed, with a cephalic index of 76, which makes them of mesaticephalic type (*see* p. 49). The same physical stock lived at Worlebury Camp, at the west end of the trackway on the Mendips, and in Romano-British times in the villages of Woodcuts, Rotherley, and Woodyates, in Cranborne Chase, down to Saxon times.

At Glastonbury their fears held true, and some little time before the Roman occupation final disaster descended on the village, and they were put to the sword: perhaps by the Belgic invaders, who were long-heads, but of an altogether tougher fighting breed. Caesar (*Com.* v, c. 43) tells us how the Nervii, when attacking Cicero's camp, set fire to the thatch of the huts, by discharging red-hot clay sling bullets. Many of these were found at Glastonbury, and help us to visualize the final scene. We have noted that very few arms were found in the excavations, and the little dark men only wanted to be left quietly alone, and be allowed to get on with their work; and this is what they did until they were discovered. Then their outlying possessions and crops would have been destroyed, and the village surrounded. The Glastonbury men could only have watched the scene, in shuddering misery, from behind their stockades, and then the invaders, using perhaps the dug-outs they had collected from the waterside, would have paddled across the lake, and discharging their red-hot clay bullets have fired the thatch. When the flames subsided, the few survivors would have been put to the sword. Yet the little dark men have had their revenge; from the very start of their career they appear to have lived in communities; it may have been a tradition they brought with them from the shores of the Mediterranean. The Belgae who oppressed them, like the later Anglo-Saxons, whom they resembled, preferred a more open-air life, and today their fair-haired descendants have the same tastes.

Professor Fleure, in his paper on the *Racial History of the British People*, sums up the matter thus: "These descendants of the Neolithic people are the long-headed, long-faced, dark-haired, brown-eyed people that form so strong an element of the

THE EARLY IRON AGE

population of big English cities. They seem better able than all other types to withstand slum conditions, so that in the second generation of great city life they have arisen in their millions to form once more, after many days, almost a majority, perhaps, of the population of south Britain." So the tale of the Mediterranean men is not yet completed.

Having seen something of men's houses in the Early Iron Age and the more domestic details of their lives, we can turn to their larger works. The trackways, or road system, link up a series of splendid earthworks, and many of these are of Iron Age construction. Starting perhaps as simple cattle enclosures, surrounded by a ditch and bank, with some additional precautions, taken at the entrances, these camps were gradually improved, until we arrive at such a masterpiece as Maiden Castle near Dorchester. More banks were added, the entrances made into mazes of ingenuity, and the whole developed just in the same way as the Tower of London, where we find the Norman keep surrounded by much later works.

It is very difficult to estimate the age of earthworks, especially the very simple ones. In some, Roman coins have been found, but this would not justify us in saying that an earthwork was Roman. The Romans fortified their camps when on the march, but did not often occupy the Iron Age hill forts. Roman coins in these may point to the times of the Saxon terror, when the Britons fled to these forts as places of refuge and took their money with them.

Earthworks are classified by archaeologists as A, Promontory Fortresses, where a piece of high ground inaccessible by reason of precipices or water on one side, has been defended by artificial works on the other. B 1 are Hilltop Forts with artificial defences following the natural lines of the hill, and are sometimes called Contour Forts. B 2 are forts on high ground, less dependent on natural slopes for protection, and there are later types which do not concern us now.

It may be well to give first a brief description of the terms used in describing an earthwork. Vallum, rampart, and agger, all mean earthen walls. Fosse or ditch, an escarpment is the outer slope, while the counterscarp is the inner slope; if the counterscarp is brought up above the level line as a smaller rampart,

HILL FORTS

this is a revetment. The flat piece of undisturbed ground between the ramparts is a berm. The plans of earthworks, which generally look like hairy caterpillars biting their tails, show the top of a slope as a thick line tapering off down the slope.

Now as to the way the builders went to work. To start with, they had as good an eye for the possibilities of a piece of country as a Royal Engineer officer, or a fox-hunting squire. They always chose pleasant sunny situations where the thyme-scented grass gave good feeding for their cattle, and the scabious flowers nodded in the breeze to the song of the skylark. There is no more pleasant place in which to loaf than an old earthwork; you can always get into the sun and out of the wind, and the slope of the banks is exactly right for an easy position from which to gaze over the countryside, and that is just what the old men wanted to do. Their cattle would have grazed on the hillside, meanwhile the watchman kept a look out for wolves and wild boar, or wandering cattle-lifters. Cattle were wealth in those days.

The builders then chose the rounded hump of a chalk down, which was not controlled by any higher ground, and it is probable that the first thing they did was to dig one simple ditch and bank, or fosse and vallum. They doubtless carried up the chalk in rough baskets, and so raised the bank above them. On examining an old earthwork, the first thing to do is to discover the natural level, and then see how they went to work, because at first sight the fosses are so deep, and the banks so high, that it seems impossible such work could have been done without steam navvies. When we have found the natural level we discover that the art of the job was that, by the basket of earth dug out, not only was the ditch lowered, but the bank raised, and that a higher bank was made more speedily on a slope than on the level. Again, on a very steep slope the soil dug out could be thrown downhill.

Still, notwithstanding all this, these earthworks must have been tremendous undertakings. The outermost of the three banks at Badbury, near Wimborne, Dorset, is one mile in circuit; at Maiden Castle, near Dorchester, nearly $1\frac{1}{3}$ miles. Particular care was given to the design of the entrances. At Badbury there are two, one on the east and the other west. On the west side the banks have been cut through in other places in recent

THE EARLY IRON AGE

times, but originally any invading force had to enter by these two ways, which left it very much at the mercy of the bowmen on the banks above them. A "flanking" entrance was so arranged that the right side (unprotected by shield) was exposed to the defenders' arrows. The tops of the banks were palisaded, and the bottoms of the ditches were perhaps filled with sharpened stakes. The wide areas between the banks, called "berms", may have been used as cattle pens—a stampede of half-wild cattle at night would not have been pleasant—or, as at Maiden Castle, the camp may have been divided into two parts for the same purpose.

Hut circles are found in the earthworks, which suggest huts as shown in our drawings. Heaps of sling stones have been found, and bracers, or wrist-guards, which show that bows were used.

There has been considerable discussion as to how the Hill Fort men provided themselves with water, and there are various theories. First, it must be remembered that the fort formed the citadel, and place of refuge for the district, and the people grouped themselves around it. Their little huts were not difficult to make, and their simple husbandry meant only the cultivation of the terraces, or lynchets, on the hillside where they grew their corn; they did not need or use so much water as we do today, and in the usual way were free to go downhill to the nearest stream. However, at Maiden Castle, excavation revealed an intricate system of tunnels and gutters on the chalk floor converging on certain pits. These pits may have been lined with sewn skins to make watertight cisterns and the gutters possibly puddled with clay so that these hill forts could be supplied with water in time of seige. Then there is the dew pond, which is still used to water cattle on the Wiltshire Downs. This is made as fig. *152*. A shallow saucerlike depression is cut in the chalk, and

152 A dew pond

WATER SUPPLY AND DEW PONDS

lined with straw. On this comes a layer of puddled clay, with rims of chalk to protect the clay from the feet of cattle. Loose flints are put on the bottom, and the pond is started with a little water in it. The straw and clay cut off the heat of the earth, and when the moist mists drive over the Downs at night and come to the cooler pond, they condense on its surface. Ordinary ponds are formed in this way, where a pocket of clay comes in a warmer soil. Water drains into it, and the cattle puddle up the clay till it is free from cracks and watertight, and so the pond extends.

In the hot summer of 1921 we were going through Dorset looking at earthworks, and found the pond on the top of Holt Heath, near Bull Barrow, full of water, while the Tarrant river in the valley close by was absolutely dry. The Wycombe chairmakers, who go into the woods to turn chair legs, obtain water in an ingenious way. If you examine the bole of a beech tree you will find well-marked channels where the rain and condensed dew runs down the tree-trunk. The chairmaker makes a cross cut in such a channel, and drives in a chip of wood which diverts the water into a pail; turning on a tap is not the only way to get water.

The concentration of a number of people either making or living in a hill fort was to have great results. In the old days, the hunting tribe was like a large family, who very speedily knew all one another's good points, and were so apt to emphasize the bad ones; life was not at all exciting. Here there must have been a bustling life, with all kinds of men coming and going, and new things to be discovered. Customs would arise, and Law solidify out of these. Language would develop around the hut fires, and traditional tales form the beginnings of literature. These hill forts are evidences of a more ordered system of life than anything which had gone before; even today with our transport system, and organized labour, the construction of either Badbury or Maiden Castle would call for concentrated effort. To make a flint or metal implement, which you do yourself, is one thing; to construct a camp which needs the labour of many men is quite another. It had to be planned; there must have been some few men who were skilled in the design of camps, and could say to the tribesmen, "Today we will cut this ditch, and dump

153 Coracles

HILL FORT SOCIETY AND WARFARE

the stuff here to form a bank. You are going wrong there; and you have not allowed sufficient room for that escarpment, because the angle of repose at which chalk will come to rest is flatter than that", and so on.

If our readers read Mr. Hippisley Cox's book, *The Green Roads of England*, they will find how these hill forts are all linked up on a trackway system, as well adapted to the needs of the time as the Roman roads and stations later on. This road question brings up fortification, and what it means. Let us imagine Badbury, not grass grown as it is today but all shining white where the chalk banks had been thrown up; or Maiden Castle, 1½ miles round its outer circuit. It must have been startlingly formidable in appearance. As the later tribes came in as immigrants, and found their way along the trackways, these hill forts were there to bar their way. Of course, there were not any invading armies in those days, who needed to maintain lines of communication with the coast; the invaders were tribes who wished to settle down. In the case of hostile tribes, they certainly could not afford to cross a trackway and leave a hill fort on their flank or rear, unless they came to terms with its inhabitants. In this way these hill forts played exactly the same part as the Norman Castles and walled towns of the Middle Ages.

We have seen how fond the ancient Britons were of wattlework, and on p. 192 how it was used even for the construction of churches. Boats were made in this way, and fig. *153* shows a coracle, of which the wattled framework was covered with hide; coracles are still in occasional use by fishermen on Welsh rivers. Primitive peoples frequently make boats in this way. Fig. *154* shows the framework of the umiak, or women's boat of the Eskimo, made of driftwood, laced together with thongs, without a single nail, and covered with skins; and fig. *155* how it is fitted with a mast, and square sail of membrane. Later Bronze Age

154   Framework of umiak

THE EARLY IRON AGE

155 Eskimo umiak

or Iron Age rock engravings from Europe show a heavy seagoing vessel like a Viking Long Ship, with a high curved stern and an animal totem at the prow. Everyone in these boats seems to be rowing furiously (*156*). Fig. *157* shows swords of the Early Iron Age: 1 shows an early Halstatt pattern, and 2 a later La Tène type shown in scabbard. The scabbards were in bronze, and frequently ornamented with very beautiful designs. The sword blade was of iron, with a tang on to which was fitted a bronze mount to the handle, the latter formed of bone or wood threaded on to the tang.

Fig. *157* also

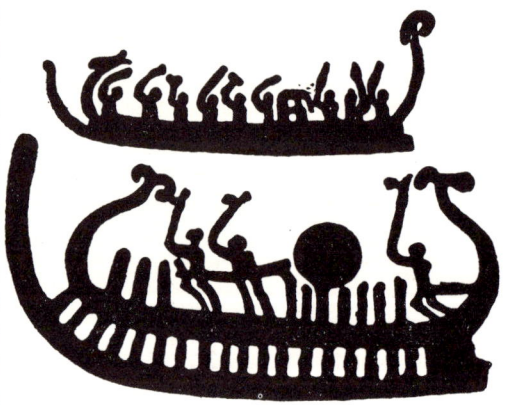

156 Rock engraving of two Bronze or Iron Age war vessels

SHIPS AND SWORDS

shows two iron spear-heads of the same period which are rather different from the leaf-shaped patterns of the Bronze Age. The shields were now oblong in shape. This splendid work of art can be seen at the British Museum, and is made of bronze decorated with enamels. This form of decoration appears to have developed out of the use of coral, added as an ornament to bronze.

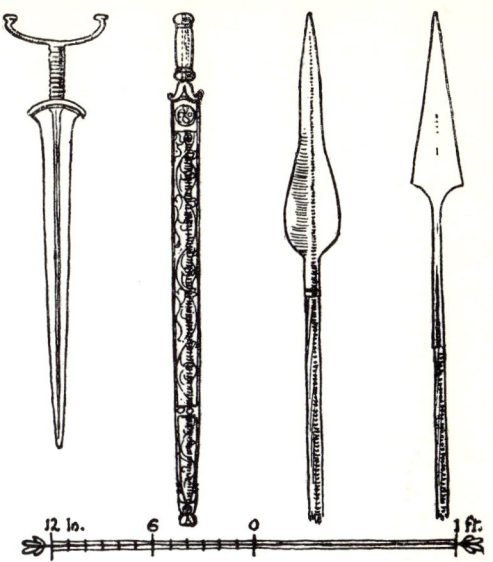

157 Early Iron Age swords and spears

Then Early Iron Age metalworkers made studs, with an enamel surface, and pinned these to the bronze. This led the way to the crowning glory of their work, Champlevé enamelling. Here the field of the design was graved out of the metal, and the ground being first scored to give a key was filled in with the fused enamel, which, being polished, was finished flush with the face. Fig. *158*, of an enamelled harness ornament, shows to what mastery of line the designers had now advanced. Think of the splendid appearance of an Early Iron Age chieftain; his helmet, shield, and horse-mountings all bronze, not dull as now but shining like gold, with the enamels afire like liquid rubies. The earliest enamels were of one colour, red.

158 Enamelled harness ornament

In the Early Iron Age, costume had developed and weaving in brilliant colours was practised. It is thought that these were combined into primitive tartans. As

THE EARLY IRON AGE

159 Two Scythian men wearing trousers, drawn on an Iron Age vessel

in the Bronze Age, a piece of material was folded around the body, in the form of a kilt, and this with a sleeveless vest, and a cloak which was semicircular in shape, completed a man's attire. The shoes were cut out of hide, with straps attached, and gathered round the ankle. The Brythons appear to have introduced the loose trousers, which originated with the Persians and Scythians (*159*). The women wore a long tunic reaching to the ankles, with short sleeves. Women, men, and horses, all alike, wore beautiful torcs, belts, and brooches, of bronze and enamel.

Another thing which was not found at Glastonbury was the burial-place, so that we do not know what objects they buried with their dead; fortunately for archaeologists, there are many other Early Iron Age cemeteries also belonging to the Marnian Celts where this information can be gained. A very important one is at Arras, near Market Weighton, in the East Riding of Yorkshire; here the barrows are small, circular in form, not more than 2 feet high by about 8 feet diameter. The body was not cremated but buried in a very contracted position in a cist, or grave cut in the chalk. The skulls show the people to have been long-headed (*dolichocephalic*), and here for the first time iron is found with the body. This means either that there had been a reversion to the old burial customs of the Neolithic people, or that these were introduced afresh from the Continent; in any case the cremation of the Bronze Age passes away. Again, the

CHARIOT BURIALS

long-headed skulls may point to a survival of Neolithic people, who had absorbed the old round-headed Bronze Age invaders, or to fresh invasions from the Continent. Some of the barrows at Arras and elsewhere in Yorkshire, were found to contain the remains of chariots, and these resemble the chariot burials in France; this rather points to the Yorkshire barrows being the work of invaders. The tyres of the chariots there are about 2 feet 8 inches in diameter, and parts of the oak rims or fellies were found, mortised for as many as sixteen spokes. There were nave collars, for the hubs, of iron plated with bronze, and the skeletons of horses of about thirteen hands. We saw the beginnings of chariots at Heathery Burn Cave in the Bronze Age, and it is obvious that by the time of the Early Iron Age these played an important part in everyday life. Many of the Yorkshire barrows suggest that women were buried in them. In one were found one hundred glass beads of a beautiful deep blue colour, ringed and spotted with white; others were of clear green glass with a white line. There were rings of amber and gold, and bracelets of bronze. In the mounds were broken pottery, and the bones of animals, and charcoal, as if there had been a funeral feast. An iron mirror was found at Arras, very much rusted of course. Fig. *160* shows one of bronze of a more usual type.

Fig. *162* shows late Celtic ornament. We saw by fig. *124* how the Bronze Age peoples' patterns were chevrons, lozenges, and concentric circles, and the Early Iron Age saw the introduction of the curve, and the endless possibilities which come about through combinations of curves.

We can now pass on to the latest type of burials in this country, and there is but little doubt that these were the work of Belgic invaders. They were discovered in 1886, at Aylesford in Kent. This was in the Belgic country, and

160   The Bronze mirror

THE EARLY IRON AGE

161　A potter's wheel

here we find that cremation had again been introduced, and the Belgae appear to have maintained this custom.

　The cist, or grave, covered by a barrow, had passed out of fashion, and its place had been taken by a circular pit, about 3 feet 6 inches deep, the sides and bottom of which were daubed with chalky clay. In the pit were found burnt bones, and the fragments of the pottery cinerary urns, in which there had been placed a pail, flagon, skillet, or shallow saucepan, and brooches

WHEEL-MADE POTTERY

all of bronze. The custom evidently still persisted of burying objects which had belonged to the dead, because it had some symbolical meaning; or for their use in the spirit world; or because it would have been unlucky to retain the objects in everyday use. The flagon of a very beautiful shape must have been imported from Italy.

The Aylesford pottery marks a great advance. It is of very graceful shape, and must have been turned on a wheel, and given a lustrous black surface in the firing. The wheel may have been of the turn-table type described on p. 197, and shown at A in fig. *161*, or the potters may have advanced as far as the wheel shown at B. This is a very primitive type, which was used until lately for making flower-pots and bread-pans.

Except for this important detail of the reintroduction of cremation, the Belgae do not seem to have effected any very great alteration in the everyday life of the times. They were a fierce fighting people, and conquered the south-eastern districts. This gave them possession of the iron mines of the Sussex Weald, which was to be the Black Country of England until the eighteenth century.

The Brythons and the older Goidelic stock of the Bronze

162 Celtic patterns

THE EARLY IRON AGE

Age, and the Marnian Celts at Glastonbury and Arras, learned to use iron but continued to live their lives in their own way.

There are still a great many things which remain a puzzle to the archaeologist about the everyday doings of all those people who lived here before the coming of the Romans, when our written story began. Prominent among them is how they managed for communications and transport. It was seen (p. 144) how the stones forming the inner ring at Stonehenge, each weighing many tons, were brought all the way from Prescelly Mountains on the Pembrokeshire coast. This, as the crow flies, is about 150 miles. How could such a feat of transportation have been accomplished in 2000 B.C.? Either they were brought by land, making a wide détour to avoid the Severn Estuary, when thick virgin forest and wide marshes covered so much of the lower ground, or they must have come by sea, starting in the open Atlantic, weathering the rocky promontory of Cornwall, and beating up the chops of the English Channel. Yet we know nothing of their ships and very little of their roads, though a few of the many ancient trackways on the higher ground show some evidence of having been in use as early as the time of the Bronze Age population. And why bring those great stones at all? Were they moved in slow stages as holy indispensables in a tribal migration as the Ark of the Covenant was carried by the Israelites in the Bible? Or was it a mystical act of conquest such as prompted Edward the First to take the Stone of Scone from Scotland to London? Or was it that Prescelly Top was regarded as more sacred than Salisbury Plain and the transfer of its rock regarded as sanctifying the great shrine—just as we sometimes have water from the Jordan brought over here for christenings.

The tracks which run along the crests of the chalk downlands and the Cotswold Hills all go over ground which has been less disturbed by the building and agricultural operations which have altered the face of this densely populated country during the Middle Ages and the more strenuous later times. For that reason they were used by the cattle-drovers right down to the end of the last century. So they have been well preserved and are well marked.

But the Bronze Age people were scattered all over the country

TRACKWAYS AND SETTLEMENTS

and the uniform evenness of their culture indicates that they must have had a fair system of communications, if only by bridle-paths. Recent archaeological research in Sussex has revealed the presence of Bronze Age farms, and one observes that the roadways leading to these were fair-sized tracks and not mere bridle-paths.

As to the Iron Age, it is most likely that there were paved roads. A settlement was excavated in Anglesey where a road of this kind and apparently of ancient date went right through its midst. And not far from the same place, in 1942, a most remarkable find was made of a quantity of iron tyres belonging to chariot-wheels. But if there were roads, even indifferent ones, there remains the problem as to who maintained them. That means a higher order of civilization than we usually credit our prehistoric ancestors with. Still, we must remember that the Bronze Age seems to have had more than a thousand years of peace, and if the tribes of the Iron Age were sufficiently well organized to make such vast earthworks as at Maiden Castle and Old Oswestry they may have maintained some sort of roads in the pauses between intertribal hostilities. Besides, in many things they imitated the Romans who were making such a stir with their conquests and their new way of things on the Continent. So that when the Caesars arrived they had little difficulty in attracting the populations of the hillforts into Romanized tribal centres.

Camulodunum, or Colchester, was the chief town of the Trinovantes; Verulamium, or St. Albans, of the Catuvellauni, and Cassivellaunus was their king. Caesar is supposed to have referred to St. Albans, when he wrote of "an oppidum with the Britons is a place amidst dense forest, fortified by a rampart or ditch, whither it is their habit to assemble to escape an enemy's raid". Corinium (Cirencester) was the home of the Dobuni; Calleva (Silchester) of the Atrebates; London of the Cantii. Women were allowed to be Queens. Cartismandua was Queen of the Brigantes, and their country was the Pennines, and Boudicca (Boadicea) Queen of the Iceni.

In the Bronze Age chapter we discussed trade and traffic (p. 176); and this brings up the question of money or the currency which is used as a medium for that exchange of goods which is

THE EARLY IRON AGE

163   Currency bars

the basis of Trade. It has been suggested that the gold bracelets of the Bronze Age may have been used as money; these have been found with rings fastened to them, and are called ring-money, and the idea does not seem too wildly remote. This is hardly the case with fig. *163*, which illustrates iron currency bars, and we can imagine our readers, unless they are born financiers, saying, "How on earth could anyone buy anything with a kind of iron walking stick." We are quite sure that many have been puzzled by the various methods which have been adopted by different peoples. There was the British sovereign of gold, now unhappily not in general use; its dirty greasy successor, so typical of the time, the Treasury note; one has heard of cowrie-shells, and so on; in all parts of the world different things seem to be used, but none so odd perhaps as the iron bars of the Early Iron Age.

Of the two currency bars found at Glastonbury, one is $27\frac{7}{8}$ inches long, and weighs 4666 grains, the other, $21\frac{1}{4}$ inches, but much thicker than number one, weighs 9097 grains. Mr. Reginald Smith has identified currency bars with the *taleae ferreae* of Caesar (*De Bello Gallico* v, 12), and it is thought that there were six varieties, the British unit being about 4770 grains. Bars of $\frac{1}{4}$, $\frac{1}{2}$, 1, $1\frac{1}{2}$, 2 and 4 units have been identified.

Perhaps we can give an illustration which will show how these things become accepted as currency. In remote villages in this country not long ago, it was usual to have a settling-up day once a year after harvest; during the rest of the year the people ran bills, which they chalked up on the barn door. At settling time the farmer would go to the miller and say, "How do we stand", to which the miller replied, "I have ground your corn,

CURRENCY

and you had some of the flour, but I sold the remainder, and owe you £5." The miller went to the baker who said, "Yes, I had my flour from you, but supplied you with bread, and owe you £5." The butcher bought his beasts from the farmer, but sold his meat to all the village, and so they weighed up the matter, and came to a settlement. It is quite conceivable that the same £5 note, with a little small change, would have passed from hand to hand, and enabled the village to start on another year's trading all square; if instead of the £5 note, you had an iron bar, it really did not matter so much—in fact it was rather better, because like our extinct gold sovereign, it was a thing of value itself, which is more than can be said of the Treasury note. Intertribal and international trade, though more complicated, was, and still is, conducted on this same basis, of the exchange of commodities. It is well to remember this, when so large a part of what is called business today is in reality only a gamble with the product of other men's labour. Real wealth springs from mother earth, and real work is to be engaged in winning or shaping her treasures.

We find a less extraordinary currency than the iron bars, about 150 to 200 B.C., in a British gold coinage of modern type of two values. This appears to have started in the south-east and as some of these coins are inscribed, it shows that writing had progressed.

The unit system of the currency bars is proof of some system of weights and measures, and another is given by the beautiful pots, bowls, and metal work. A good craftsman does not make a thing to just any odd size. Use will have shown him what is the handiest weight, and the best size. A modern brick, for example, is of the size and weight that experience has shown the bricklayer can handle. Endless experiment has gone to prove this, and all the other details of everyday work and the tallies or the sticks, which were kept as a reminder, became in time recognized standards and measurements.

The currency bars are proof of the exchange of commodities, but do not help us to understand how values were fixed; how much corn a plough was worth. With such necessaries of life, the plough was worth the extra amount of corn the farmer could grow by its use; that would be its just price in theory. In practice it is often regulated by scarcity, which tends to increase the price of the plough, or by overproduction, when the price of ploughs

THE EARLY IRON AGE

goes down. Then there are luxuries, for which people will pay more than they are worth, because they are beautiful, or very scarce, and so on. All this wants to be borne in mind; we shall find how in the Middle Ages, Canon Law was very much concerned with the Just Price and Usury, and even today a profiteer is not held to be a very pleasant person. Trade and currency bars; weights and measures; the honesty of the good man, and even the thieving of the rogue, are part of that wonderful peepshow into the past we call History, and cannot be neglected.

Now as we are approaching the end of our space, it may be as well to see if we can discover anything of the animating spirit which inspired these people, and gave savour to their everyday life. We saw in Neolithic times how men are thought to have worshipped the powers of Nature, with a great Mother God over all. Gildas, a monk, writing in the sixth century A.D., said: "Nor will I cry out upon the mountains, fountains, or hills, or upon the rivers, which now are subservient to the use of men, but once were an abomination and destruction to them, and to which the blind people paid divine honour." Yet Nature worship still lingers with stones which are lucky, and wells whose waters are curative.

Sun worship appears to have been typical of the early Bronze Age, and with the arrival of the Celts may have taken the form of hero worship. It is probable that in the Early Iron Age, as the gods became more personal and intimate, they took to themselves as well the failings of man; as they were stronger and braver than man, in the perpetual warfare they waged with the powers of darkness, so also they were more cruel and hard.

Druidism appears to have been the religion of the later Celtic tribes of Britain and Gaul, but doubtless it was grafted on to the Hero and Sun worship of the Bronze Age, and the older Nature and Moon worship of the Neolithic man. This has been a very general practice; a conquering people would be willing to place the credit of the victory to the power of their own gods, yet unwilling to neglect the ones who had been overthrown. A god was a god, even when associated with defeat, and might easily revenge himself by alliance with the powers of Darkness. It was wiser then not to run any risks, so we find old faiths adapted to new religions.

DRUIDS

Caesar in *De Bello Gallico*, book vi, gives us an interesting picture of Druids and Druidism, and other sources of inspiration are the Celtic Myths and Legends that Mr. Squire has gathered together in his book. These tales have come down to us, because they were gathered together by monkish chroniclers, from the twelfth to the fifteenth centuries, but for all the time before that they had been traditional in the Celtic countries, since the days when they were first recited by Druidical bards to the accompaniment of harps.

Caesar wrote of the Druids: "As one of their leading dogmas, they inculcate this: that souls are not annihilated, but pass after death from one body to another, and they hold that by this teaching men are much encouraged to valour, through disregarding the fear of death. They also discuss and impart to the young many things concerning the heavenly bodies and their movements, the size of the world and our earth, natural science, and of the influence and power of the immortal gods." Again quoting Caesar: "The whole Gaulish nation is to a great degree devoted to superstitious rites; and on this account those who are afflicted with severe diseases, or who are engaged in battles and dangers, either sacrifice human beings for victims, or vow that they will immolate themselves, these employ the Druids as ministers for such sacrifices, because they think that, unless the life of man be repaid for the life of man, the will of the immortal gods cannot be appeased. Others make wicker-work images of vast size, the limbs of which they fill with living men and set on fire."

From the little that is known, it can be gathered that the Druids formed a religious aristocracy, to which entrance could only be gained by a long novitiate. There was a Head, or Pope, elected for life; they were exempt from war and taxation; acted as judges, and had a monopoly of learning. Time was reckoned by nights, and the year counted by the revolutions of the moon. White bulls were sacrificed before the mistletoe was cut from the sacred oak. Captives were killed, and signs read from the flow of their blood, and the palpitation of their entrails.

The Gaulish Druids looked to their British brethren, as possessed of a purer faith, and novices were sent here to learn the mysteries. This came about because the Continent fell under the influence of Rome at an earlier date than we did; for the

THE EARLY IRON AGE

same reason, with the advent of the Romans here, Druidism was driven into the West, because its practices shocked even the Romans, until they finally routed it out of its headquarters in Anglesey. It survived in Ireland, which never fell under the Roman influence, until St. Patrick overthrew Cromm Cruaich.

If the Celtic legends are poisoned by hints of awful cruelty, we must yet remember that it was not the cruelty of the Romans, who enjoyed the killing in the Amphitheatre, but the religion of sacrifice carried to its most awful conclusion. The Druids were not cruel for cruelty's sake, but to propitiate the gods.

On the other side of the picture, we have the pleasant fact that the Celtic myths and legends, becoming traditional, were handed down, and became in the hands of the monkish chroniclers the foundation on which has been built a literature that is entirely our own.

We have seen what great artists the Celts were, when they turned to handicraft; their metal work, and enamels, have been the inspiration of many an artistic revival, hailed as new, and yet in reality just as old as the Druids.

The great Celtic festivals were Beltane at the beginning of May, Midsummer Day, the Feast of Lugh in August, and Samhain. We still have survivals of these in May Day, St. John's Day, Lammas, and Hallow-e'en or All Saints, and the bonfires around which we dance on joyful occasions started life as the sacrificial pyres on which victims were burned to propitiate the gods, or cattle offered to stay the ravages of a murrain, or plague, at the original Celtic festivals.

INDEX

The numerals in **heavy type** denote the **figure numbers** of the illustrations.

Abbeville, 29, 40, 42
 Man, 42, 55
Abbevillian flint axes, 38, 40; **9-11**
Abraham, 114, 146
Achaeans, 150, 176
Acheulean Man, 32, 48, 55
 flint hand-axe, 39; **8, 12, 13**
 flint scraper, 42; **14**
 Period, 36, 48
Achilles, 146, 168
Adige, River, 176
Adriatic, 176
Adze, 195; **147**
Africa, 149
 South, 39
Afridis, 175
Agamemnon, 175
 Tomb of, 137
Agger, 202
Agriculture, 99, 115, 134, 135, 192; **122, 123, 137**
Aichbuhl, Neolithic house at, 131; **84, 85**
Alaska, 92
Alexander the Great, 175
Alfred, King, 117
Alpera cave paintings, 85
Alpine people, 118
Altamira Cave, wall-paintings in, 80, 84, 89, 99; **43-6, 61**
Anchor, 192; **144**
Anglesey, 178, 220
Arabia, 172
Archery, 78
Arctic hare, 101
Ariège, 106
Ark of the Covenant, 214
Arminghall stone circle, 148
Armlet, jet, **155**
Arras (East Riding), 210, 214
Arrow-head, bone, 89; **50**
 chisel-ended, 106; **68**
 flint, 86, 89, 128; **47, 83**

Art, prehistoric, 79-84, 89, 99-102, 108 165, 176, 209, 211; **1, 42-6, 51, 52, 61-5, 70-3, 78, 124, 158, 162**
Arunta tribe (Australia), 67
Aryan peoples, 123, 161, 175
Atrebates, 215
Aurignac Man, Chap. IV, 102, 175
 his art, 79; **42-6**
Australian aborigines, 44, 62-70, 85, 94, 179; **27-33**
 family relationships, 68
Austria, 172, 181
Avalon, Isle of, 185
Avebury, Neolithic religious sanctuary at, 67
Avon, River, 178
Awl, 107
Axe, Bronze, 151; **106, 107**
 Chalk, 148
 Danish midden, **74**
 hand-, 33, 39, 40, 42, 60; **9-12**
 Iron Age, 200
 See also Celt
Aylesford, Kent, 175, 211, 213

Badbury, 203, 205
Bahia Blanca, 77
Barb, invention of the, 90; **50**
Barrow, 210
 bell, 166; **126**
 bowl, 166; **126**
 disc, 166; **126**
 long, 136; **95**
 round, 149, 156
Beaker people, 120, 148, 165, 176, 177
Bears, 115
 cave-, 60

Beavers, 115
Beazeley, Alex., 200
Belerium (Land's End), 177, 178
Belfort Gap, 176
Belgae, 113, 124, 182, 201, 211, 213
Bellows, 194
Beltane, 220
Berkshire, 118, 179
Berm, 165, 203, 204
Bill-hook, 195; **140**
Bird dart, eskimo, 94; **55**
Bison, 84, 101
 wall-painting of, 99; **61**
Blackdown Hills, 116
Bladder dart, Eskimo, 93; **55**
Blade cores, Palaeolithic, 72, 73; **34**
Blades, flint, 73; **35**
Boat, Bronze Age toy, **132**
Bodkins, bone, 77
Bolas, 61
Bone implements, 87, 88, 149; **48**
 arrow-heads, 89; **50**
 needles, 78, 87, 94; **48**
Borers, 86
Bos longifrons, 115
Boucher de Perthes, M., 29
Boudicca (Boadicea), 215
Bow and arrow, 78, 85
 See also Arrow-head
Bow drill, 78, 102, 127; **41**
Bracelet, 85, 198, 200
Bracer (wristguard), 204
Brachycephalic, 49
Brandon, Norfolk, 179
Bread, 134
Breastplate, Bronze Age gold, **79**
Brenner Pass, 176
Breuil, Abbé, 80
Bridge, 162; **121**
Bridle-bit, Bronze Age, 155, 160
 Iron Age, 193

221

INDEX

Brigantes, 215
British East Africa, 43
British Museum, 39, 63, 64, 66, 94, 124, 132, 151, 155
Britons, 124
Brittany, 120, 177
Broch, 138
Bronze, 150, 151
Bronze Age, 116, 120, 138, 147, 148, Chap. VII
  axes,, 151; **106, 107**
  breastplate, **79**
  brooch, 155; **111**
  clothes, 159; **116, 130, 131**
  implements, 151; **106–11**
  ornament, 165, 176; **78, 124**
  razor, 160; **117**
  ship bowl, **133**
  smith, 155; **110**
  spear-heads, 152; **108**
  swords, 153, 155; **109**
  toy boat, **132**
  tumuli, 166, 170; **126–9**
Brooch, 155, 195, 196; **111, 149, 150**
Bryn Celli Dhu, 170; **127–9**
Brythons, 113, 124, 182, 210, 213
Bucket, Bronze Age, 155
Bull barrow, 205
Bulleid, Mr. Arthur, 185, 195
Burial, 166, 210, 211
Burins, or chisels, flint, 77; **36, 37**
Bushmen, 85, 99

Cadiz, 177
Caesar, 177, 178, 201, 215, 219
Caithness, 118, 138
Calleva, 215
Cambridgeshire, 130
Camps, Neolithic, 136; **76**
Camulodunum, 215
Cannibalism, 47, 61, 67
Canoe, bark, 65; **32**
  dug-out, 116, 192; **75, 143**
Canterbury, 174
Cantii, 215
Carcassone Gap, 120
Cardiganshire, 178
Carnarvonshire, 178
Carpathians, 33, 172
Cartismandua, Queen, 215
Cassiterides, 177

Cassivellaunus, 215
Cattle, 115, 135, 136, 203
Catuvellauni, 215
Causeway camps, 136
Cave bear, 60
Cave-dwellers, the first, Chap. III; **24**
Celt (axe)
  stone, 120, 125, 149; **81, 82**
Celtic Festivals, 220
  fields, **137**
  hill figures, **138**
  ornament, 211; **162**
  shield, **136**
Celts (race), 123, 124, 149, 166, 176, 181, 200, 210, 214, 218
Cephalic index, 49
Cevennes, 120
Chalk axes, 148
Châlons, 176
Chamonix, 30
Chariots, Bronze Age, 160–2, 211; **118–20**
  Iron Age, 211
Chelles, 61
Cherbourg, 178
Chile, 78, 99
Chilterns, 117
Chisels or gravers, **36, 37**
Christchurch, 178
Cicero, 201
Cirencester, 215
Cissbury, 124, 179
Clacton, 52
Clapham, 31
Clapper bridge, 162; **121**
Clothes, Bronze Age, 159; **116, 130, 131**
  Iron Age, 209, 210; **159, 160**
  Neolithic, 132
Coinage, 193, 216, 217; **163**
Colchester, 215
Coldrum monument, 115
Comb, weaver's, 159; **115**
Commont, M., 60
Contour forts, 202
Copper, 178
Coracle, 66, 207; **153**
Corbilo, 177, 178
Corduroy roads, 162
Corinium, 215
Corn grinding, 192; **145**
Cornish, 124
Cornwall, 116, 177, 214
Cotswolds, 118, 214
Counterscarp, 202
Cowrie shells, 108

Cox, David, 187
Cox, Mr. Hippisley, *The Green Roads of England*, 207
Cranborne Chase, 201
Cranhogs, 182
Craven Arms, 178
Cremation, 106, 165, 166, 167, 168, 175, 212
Creswell Caves, 43
Crags, 86
Cretaceous beds, 60
Cretans, 175
Crô-Magnon, 57, 108, 112
Cromlech, 139; **100**
Cromm Cruach, 220
Crucibles, fireclay, 193
Cultivation, 99, 115, 134, 135, 164, 192; **122, 123, 137**
Cumberland, 176
Currency bar, 193, 216; **163**
Customs, 205

Dalcarlia, 200
Daleau, M., 100
Dancing, 85
Danes, 113, 118
Danube, 33, 172, 176
Danzig, 176
Dartmoor, 140, 162, 178
Darwin, Charles, 43–6, 48, 61, 63, 67, 77, 78, 79, 85, 98, 99, 101
Dead, disposal of the, 46, 54, 57, 61, 106, 136–8, 165, 166, 210; **95, 119**
Deer, 101, 115
  antler picks, 124; **80**
  hunt, Neolithic, **70, 71**
Denmark, 110, 176, 178
  midden axe from, 74
Derbyshire, 118
Devon, 116
Dew ponds, 204; **152**
Digging-stick, 99; **60**
Dnieper, 176
Dog, domestication of the, 107
Dolichocephalic, 49
Doll's house, Neolithic, **86**
Dolmens, 120, 139; **100**
Doon, 138
Dorchester, 116, 202, 203
Dorians, 176
Drill, 78, 102, 127; **41**
Druidism, 147, 218, 219
Dubois, Professor E., 48

222

INDEX

Dug-out canoe, 116, 192; 75, 143
Dunstable Downs, 179
Durrington, 147

Early Iron Age, 117, Chap. VIII
Earthworks, 117, 202
Eastbourne, 115
Edward I, 214
Elbe, River, 32, 176
Elephants, 42
  Elephas antiquus, 33, 42, 43
  Elephas meridionalis, 42
  Elephas primogenius, 47; **19**
"Elf-darts", 128
Elk, 60
Emu, 44
"Emu dance", 85
Ergeron, 60
Escarpment, 202
Eskimos, 66, 78, 91 et seq., 128, 179
  bow-drill, **41**
  clothing, 94
  games, 95; **56**
  houses, 138; **97, 98**
  hunting, 92–4; **53–5**
  kayak, 92; **53, 54**
  sledge, 94
  umiak, 66, 207; **154, 155**
Essex, 117
European races, 117
Evans, Sir John, *Ancient Stone Implements*, 127

Falconer, *Patagonia* (qu.), 79
Falkland Islands, 44
Falling spear (trap), 44; **17**
Farming: see Agriculture
Farnham terraces, 31; **5**
Faroe Islands, 32
Fens, the, 113, 179
Festivals, Celtic, 220
Fields, Celtic, 137
Finisterre, Cape, 177
Finnish, 123
Fire, making, 36, 65, 135; **7, 31, 89**
Fishermen, Iron Age, 192; **144**
  Mesolithic, 110
Fish-hook, 90; **50**
Fitzroy, Capt. (of the *Beagle*), 46

Fleure, Professor, 176, 201
Flinders Island, 51
Flint implements, 29, 30, 33, 36, 60; **6, 8–12, 14**
  Mesolithic, 107, 111; **68**
  Neolithic, 124, 125, 127, 133, 144; **81, 83, 90**
  Solutré, 86; **47**
  Upper Palaeolithic, 72; **34–7, 39**
Flint miners, 124, 125, 179; **80**
Food, 55, 56
Forts, 117, 202
Fosse, 202, 203
France, 172, 182
Fuegians, 45, 46, 48, 51
Funeral procession, Bronze Age, **119**

Gaelic, 18
Gaels, 176
Gainsborough, 116
Galicia, 177
Games, 95; **56**
Gauchos, 43, 44, 61
Gaul, 113, 176, 177, 185, 218
Geikie, Professor, 28
Germany, 123, 178, 182
Gibraltar, 32
Gildas (qu.), 218
Glacial Period, First, 28
  Second, 28
  Fourth, 29, 59, 79
Glaciers, 26 et seq.; **3**
Glastonbury, Church of St. Mary, 192
  lake village, 132, 151, 155, 159, 161, 182, 185, 214, 216; **139–43**
Glutton, 101
Goeree Roads, 45
Goidels, 113, 124, 181, 213
Gold, 178
Goring Gap, 116
Grain, grinding and pounding, 134, 192; **91, 92, 145**
Gravers, flint, **36, 37**
Gray's Inn Lane, flint implement found near, 39; **8**
Graz, 176
Greek, 123
Greenland, 92
Grimaldi Man, 112
Grime's Graves, 124, 125, 179; **80**

Hafting, Australian, 64; 29
Halden, Devon, 130
Hallowe'en, 220
Hallstatt, 181, 208
Hampshire, 118, 179
Hand-axes, 33, 39, 40, 42, 60; **9–12**
Harness, horse, 193
  ornament, 209; **158**
Harpoon, 91, 93; **50, 55**
Harroway, the, 179
Heathery Burn Cave, 155, 182
Hebrides, 118
Hector, 169, 175
Heidelberg Man, 50, 57
Hele stone, 145
Hellenes, 175
Hephaistos, 151
Herdsmen, 112, 114
Herefordshire, 118
Hereward the Wake, 185
Hero worship, 124, 218
Highbury, 31
Hill figures, Celtic, **138**
Hill-top forts, 202
Hippopotamus, 42; **16**
Holt Heath, 205
Homer, 169
Homo Neanderthalensis, 59
  sapiens, 72, 73
Horse, 79, 100, 101, 155 193
  (*Equus stenonis*), 42
House, Neolithic, 128–32; **84, 85**
Howe (barrow), 166
Humber, 116
Hunting, 51, 79, 81, 89, 90, 92–4, 99, 108, 115; **47, 50, 51, 53–5**
Huts, Aurignac, 38
  Australian, 65; **30**
  Eskimo, 97; **52**
  Madeleine, 95; **57, 58**
  Neolithic, 76
Huxley, 59
Hyena, 60

Ibex, wall-painting of, 108; **73**
Ice Age and its causes, 24; **2**
Ice Age, the Last, 106
  See also Glacial Periods
Iceni, 215
Icknield Way, 116, 117
Ictis, 178
Ightham, 115

INDEX

Iliad, the, 146, 151, 164, 168, 169
India, 175
Indians, American, 79, 85, 128, 150
Indo-European languages, 123
Insull, Wing-Commander, 148
Interglacial Period, Second, 30, 31, 40
Fourth, 59
Interrupted ditch camps, 126
Ireland, 176, 178, 181, 182, 220
Irish, 126
elk, 115
Iron, 150, 193
Age Man, 132; **135**
See also Early Iron Age
Iron smelting, 193; **146**
Isle of Man, 182
Isle of Wight, 113, 178
Italy, 213
Ivinghoe Beacon, 79
hills, camp on, 76
Ivory, 88, 89, 107, 149; **50**

Jason, 175
Java Ape-Man (Pithecanthropus), 48, 57; **21**
Jutland, 159

Kangaroo, 63, 67
Kayak, eskimo, 92; **53, 54**
Keller's *Swiss Lake Dwellings*, 185
Kent, 113
Kent's Cavern, Torquay, 43, 60, 89
Khyber Pass, 175
Kiev, 120, 176
Kikuyu, 134, 135, 146, 157
hut, 187; **141**
"Kimmeridge coalmoney", 198
Kitchen middens, 110
Kitscoty, 115
Knife, Iron Age, 195; **148**
Krapina, 61

Labienus, 185
La Chapelle-aux-Saints, 57, 59, 70
Laibach, 176

Lake dwellings, 132, 151, 155, 159, 161, 182, 185, 214, 216; **139-43**
Lammas, 220
Lamps, stone, 96
Lancashire, 176
Land's End (Belerium), 177, 178
Language, 48, 49, 205
Aryan, 123
La Perotte, Charente, 140
La Tène (the Shallows), 181, 196, 208
Late Celtic art, 182
Latin, 123
Lathe, Pole, 102, 120, 198; 151
Laugerie-Basse, 108
Law, 205
Leicestershire, 118
Le Moustier, 57
Levallois flakes, 61
Lever, discovery of the, 141; **102, 103**
Lincolnshire, 116, 118
Lintel, evolution of the, 120
Loess, 32, 47, 60, 86, 107, 172
Loire, River, 176, 177
Long barrows, 136; **95**
Looms, 157-9; **113, 114**
Lot, 114
Lourdes, 106
Low (barrow), 166
Lugh, feast of, 220
Lympne Flats, 113

Machairodas, *see* Sabretoothed tiger
Madeleine, La, 57, 88
Madeleine Man, 75, 87-105, 175; **1, 49, 61-5**
dwellings, 95-7; **57, 58**
Maen Hir, 120, 140; **101**
Mahsuds, 175
Maiden Castle, 116, 202-5
Maiden's bower, 117
Maidstone, 115
Main, River, 176
Malta, Stone Age temples in, 137
Mammoth, 47, 84, 101, 111; **19**
Manx, 124
March, River, 176
Marlborough Downs, 179
Marne, River, 200

Marnian Celts, 182, 200 210, 214
Marseilles, 176, 177, 178
Mas d'Azil, Caves, 106
painted pebbles at, 108; **69**
May Day, 220
Mediterranean people, 118
Medway, 115
Megaliths, 120, 139, 140, 147; **100**
Mendips, 201
Menhirs, 120, 140; **101**
Merionethshire, 177
Mersey, 178
Mesaticephalic, 49
Mesolithic Period, Chap. V
Micoque, La, 57
Migrations, Bronze Age, 172-7
Millstones, 192
Minoans, 150, 175
Mirror, bronze, 211; **160**
Mohmands, 175
Moldau, River, 176
Monolith, 140; **101**
Mont Anvers Glacier, 30
Moraines, 26; **3**
Moravia, 176
Morini, 185
Mount Carmel, 73
Moustier Man, Chap. III, 72, 79; **24**
Music, 85
Musk ox, 61, 101
Mycenae, 175

Nansen, Dr., 92
Neanderthal Man, 50, 59, 79; **25**
Necklace, 85
Needle cases, 87
Needles, bone, 78, 87, 94; **48**
Neolithic Man, 31, 64, 66, 96, 113 et seq., 179
dolls' houses, 131; **86**
houses, 128-31; **84, 85**
implements, 124-8, 133; **81-3, 90**
ovens, 132; **87, 88**
religious sanctuary at Avebury, 67
trade routes, 179
weaving pattern, **77**
worship, 145-7
Nervii, 201
Neuchâtel, Lake, 181, 196

INDEX

New Stone Age, 12, Chap. VI, 124
New Zealand, 101
Nordic Man, 118
Nördlingen, 106
Normandy, 120
Norrland (Sweden), 200
North Downs, 115, 179
Northumberland, 176
Norwegians, 118
Norwich, 148
Nuraghi, 139, 147

Oban, 106, 109
Ober-Meilen, 182
Oder, River, 176
Odysseus, 176
Old Stone Age, 23, 33, Chap. II, 112, 175
Olorgesailie, Kenya, 40
Orkneys, 118, 130, 138
Ornament. Bronze Age, 165, 176; **78, 124**
Iron Age, 209; **158**
Late Celtic, 211; **162**
Ouse, River, 116
Oven, Neolithic, 132; **87, 88**
Oxfordshire, 118
Ox-plough, 165; **122, 123**
Ox-wagons, 161

Palaeolithic Man
Lower, Chaps. I–III; 6
rock shelter, **66**
scraper, **14**
Upper, Chap. IV
Palecanthropus Palestinus, 74
Paris, 176
Patrick, Saint, 220
Patroklos, 168, 169
Paviland Cave, Wales, 85, 86
Peak District, 178
Peel, Mr., *Rough Stone Monuments*, 140
Pembrokeshire, 144, 214
Penck, Professor, 28
Peterborough, 178
Picts, 133
Picts' houses, 138; **96**
"Picts' knives", 127
Picts' tower, 139, 147; **99**
Pilgrim's Way, 115, 179
Pinsk Marshes, 120, 176
Pitfall, trap, 43; **16**

Pithecanthropus, 48, 51–3; **21**
Pitstone Hills, camps on, 76
Pleistocene, 31
Pliocene, 28, 49
Plough, 165; **122, 123**
Po Valley, 185
Pole lathe, 102, 120, 198; **151**
Posen, 176
Postbridge, 162; **121**
Potter's wheel, 102, 147, 213; **161**
Pottery, 134, 150, 165, 197; **93, 94, 125**
Prague, 176
Precession of the equinoxes, 25
Prescelly Mountains, 214
Pressburg, 176
Pressure-flaking, 72; **34**
Priam, 146, 169
Promontory forts, 202
Punjab, bamboo-straightening in the, 78
"Purgatory Hammers", 127
Pyrenees, 120
Pyrites, 133
Pythias, 177, 178

Querns, 134, 192; **91, 92, 145**

Raft, Bark, 52, 53; **22**
Rampart, 202
Razor, Bronze Age, 160; **117**
Reindeer, 61, 78, 111
"The age of the", 79
Religion, 137, 138
Revetment, 203
Rhine, 32, 176
Rhinoceros, 42, 60
tichorhinus (woolly), 47; **20**
Rhône, 176
Ridgeway, the, 179
Ring-money, 216
Rinyo, 130
River terraces, formation of, 29; **4, 5**
Roches moutonnées, 26, 28
Rock shelter, Palaeolithic, 66
Romans, 113, 147, 202, 219, 220

Rome, 176
Romney Marsh, 118
Rope, making grass, 54, 68; **23**
Rose Wood, Ightham, 11
Rotherley, 201
Routledge, Mr. and Mrs., *With a Prehistoric People*, 187
Russia, 172

Sabre-toothed tiger, 42, 43, 60; **15**
Sacrifice, human, 219
St. Acheul, 33, 42, 47, 61; **4**
St. Albans, 215
St. John's Day, 220
St. Michael's Mount, 178
St. Paul's Cathedral, 189, 190
Salmon, 90, 91; **52**
Salt, 175, 181
Samhain, 220
Sanscrit, 123
Santicola, Marcellino de, 80
Sardinia, 139, 147
Sarsen stones, 179
Sarum, 178
Saw, Iron Age, 195; **147**
Saxons, 113, 118
Schotter fields, 28
Scilly Isles, 177
Scotland, 176, 181
Scott, Sir Walter, *Redgauntlet* (qu.), 89
Scrapers, flint, 77, 86; **39**
Sculpture, Aurignac, 81, 84
Scythian men in trousers, 210; **159**
Sea routes, 177
Seals, 90, 92; **52**
Severn, River, 117
Shaft straightening, 78; **40**
Shetland Isles, 118
Shields, Iron Age, 209; **136**
Ships and sea voyages, 177, 208; **132–4, 156**
Shrewsbury, 178
Shropshire, 117
Sicily, 32
Sickness, treatment of, 54
Sickle, flint, 133; **90**
Silbury Hill, 166
Silchester, 215
Skara Brae, 130
Slaughter stone, 145
Smelting, 150, 193; **146**
Smith, Bronze Age, 110

225

INDEX

Smith, Professor G. Elliott, 48
Capt. John (qu.), 128
Solutré Man, 33, 75, 81, 86–8
  flints, 86; **47**
  needlemakers, 87; **48**
Solway, 89
Somme, River, 29, 34, 38, 59
South Downs, 116, 134, 136
Spear, Australian, 62, 63; **27, 28**
  Tasmanian, 52
Spear-head, Bronze, 152; **108**
  Madeleine, 89; **50**
  Moustier, 61; **26**
  Neolithic, 128; **83**
  Solutré, 86; **47**
Spindle, Australian, 67; **33**
  Bronze Age, 156; **112**
Spinning, 155, 198; **112**
Spiral design, Bronze Age, 176
Spokeshave, Aurignac, 77; **39**
Spoon, pottery, 135; **94**
Squire, *Celtic Myth and Legend*, 219
Staghorn, 107
Standing stone, 140, 179; **101**
Steyr, River, 28
Stockade, 117
Stone Age, Chap. II; **6**
Stone circle, 140
Stonehenge, 116, 120, 140, 144, 214; **103, 104**
Stone implements, 126; **82**
  See also Flint Implements
Stone of Scone, 214
Strike-a-light, 133; **89**
Sun discs, 167
  worship, 145, 146, 167, 218
Sussex, 118, 213
Sutherland, 138
Swanscombe Man, 50
Swedish carpenters, 200
Switzerland, 26, 30, 113, 182

Swords, 153, 208; **109, 157**
Sympathetic magic, 84

Tahitians, 54
Tartans, 209
Tasmanians, 45, 46, 51–5, 62, 67, 179; **22**
Teddington, 116
Terremare, 185
Thames, 31, 32, 34, 116, 179
Thanet, 113, 178
Tin, 151, 177, 178
"Toldos", South American, 77
Tomb of Agamemnon, 137
Totemism, 69, 84
Torquay, 43, 60, 89
Totternhoe, 117
Trackways, Prehistoric, 116, 162, 214
Trade, 108, 175, 177, 216
  routes, 172, 179
Transport, 214
Trent, River, 116
Tribe, the, 179
Trieste, 176
Trilithon, 140
Trinovantes, 215
Trousers, 210; **159**
Trumpet, 162; **121**
Tumulus, 166, 170; **127–9**
  See also Barrow
Tuyère (fireclay funnel), 194

Uffington, hill figure at, **138**
Umiak, Eskimo, 66, 207; **154, 155**
Urals, 33, 172
Ushant, 177

Vallum, 202, 203
Vannes, Morbihan, 177
Veneti, 177, 178
Venice, 185
Verulamium, 215
Vézère Valley, 57, 88, 96

Viking longships, 208
Vistula, 176

Wales, 170, 178
Wall-paintings, 79, 85, 89, 99–102, 108; **1, 42–6, 49, 51, 52, 61–5, 70–3**
Wantage, 117
War, 179
  vessels, Bronze or Iron Age, 208; **156**
Wash, the, 113, 178
Water supply, 204
Wattle-and-daub, 190
Wazirs, 175
Weald, the, 115, 118, 213
Weaving, 155–9, 198, 209; 77, **113–16**
Weights and measures, 217
Welsh, 124
Wey, river terraces of the, 31, 34, 55; **5**
Wheels, Bronze Age, 160; **118**
White Horse, the, 179
Wicklow Hills, 178
Wild boars, 110, 115
  cats, 115
Wilde, Sir Edward, 127
William of Malmesbury 190
Wind-break, 45; **18**
Wolf, 115, 165
Woodcuts (village), 201
Woodhenge, Salisbury Plain, 147; **105**
Woodyates, 201
Wootton Bassett, 178
Worcestershire, 117
Worlebury Camp, 201
Worthing, 179
Wren, Sir Christopher, 189 190
Wycombe chairmakers, 205

Yorkshire, 1. 6, 118, 156

Zürich, Lake, 182
Zuyder Zee, 176

AKIBA-SCHECHTER DAY SCHOOL
Library